CU01023727

Forms of Freedom

Paul Cudenec

Winter Oak Press, Sussex, England, 2015

winteroak.org.uk

ISBN: 978-0-9576566-5-9

CONTENTS

INTRODUCTION

There is an obvious difference between this book and the others I have written. While *The Anarchist Revelation, The Stifled Soul of Humankind* and *Antibodies* are all packed full of quotations from other writers, here there are none at all.

The reason for this lies in the nature of what I am attempting to describe. Elsewhere, it has been the history and interrelatedness of ideas that has been of primary interest to me. Describing where and how they had been expressed in various contexts was therefore a key aspect of my task. Here, on the other hand, it is not so much the *history* of the ideas that concerns me as the *ideas* themselves. I wanted to look clearly at these ideas without the clutter of the context in which they have previously been expressed.

That is not to say that I am claiming to have written this book unaided by the work of others! The influence of numerous writers will be quite apparent to the reader and the extent of the help I have received goes far beyond the selection of books in the background bibliography – for all of us are inevitably assisted in our thinking by a great diversity of sources, ranging from cinema, music or art to conversations with friends and acquaintances.

My personal involvement comes from processing all this information, working on this raw material by chipping away the irrelevancies and revealing the shape of a coherent philosophy underneath. *And what of the origins of that philosophy?* It seems to me it is something that I have not so much fashioned, as *revealed.* It was already there, in the inner structure of the rock: all I had to do was make it visible. And the more of it that I discover, the more familiar it seems to me. *It is something that I have always known,* but known in a form that could not be expressed. The more that I read, listen and discuss, the more clearly I am able to articulate that philosophy and communicate it to others. It is a lifelong process and I know I will never be able to fully grasp the whole reality, but this, at least, is an attempt to pass on what I have discovered so far.

Paul Cudenec, 2015

I

THE STREAM

A few hundred yards from where I currently live is a river. Flowing out from the river is a channelled stream, created for some local purpose that has now been forgotten.

Recently I returned here after a couple of weeks away and found, to my disappointment, that water was no longer flowing through this channel. The river had flooded in my absence and had blocked it up with silt and boulders. To start with, I was puzzled as to why the water wasn't flowing as it should. At a certain point it had difficulty in getting past a fairly small pile of stones. Without thinking about it too much, I tried moving some of these stones out of the way to let the water run. This turned out to be pointless, because these stones were not really the problem – it was the lack of general flow that meant the water was never at a high enough level to pass over them.

The reason why the flow out of the main river was diminished was all to do with the capacity at the point where the channel began. Because it was so clogged up with rubble, only a very limited depth was available to take the flow. Any excess simply brimmed over the edge and back into the river. If this top end of the channel remained shallow, because of the blockage, it was physically impossible for the water level to be any deeper further down, even where the full depth was theoretically available. The only solution was to deepen the channel right at its starting point.

As I alternated thoughts about the river with thoughts about the ideas presented in this text, I realised a metaphor was presenting itself to me. My initial reaction to the impeded flow of the channel was similar to my reaction at a younger age to the lack of freedom in our society – that is to say I noticed its absence at a point far "downstream" of the cause of the blockage. The lack of freedom we experience in our everyday lives is serious and important but merely the result of something else. To clear away the most easily-removed small objects in its path, to defend the most easily-attained liberties, will do nothing to restore the flow of real freedom in our society, although it might make our lives slightly more pleasant.

The crucial blockages are not even on a political level, where at least freedom is recognised as a desirable phenomenon. The point at which freedom is blocked is a point at which it is not even acknowledged as freedom. It is not possible to clearly see the ultimate cause of the obstruction because of the blockages and the confusion of the overspilling water between us and that point.

II

FREEDOM AND NON-FREEDOM

How can the human race embrace freedom if it does not have a clear idea of what freedom *is*? How can we ever gain a clear idea of freedom if we do not even start *looking* for it in the right places?

We might, for instance, try to discover freedom by examining the condition of non-freedom. Who in our society is universally regarded as *not free*? A prisoner in jail? A slave? Could we therefore see *not-being-in-prison* or *not-being-a-slave* as at least the starting point for being free? On a political level, maybe we could take a totalitarian system as the opposite of a free one and therefore look for freedom in the condition of *not-living-in-a-totalitarian-state* or more specifically in *not-living-under-Stalinism* or *not-living-under-Nazism*?

The problem is that by trying to define freedom in this way, we automatically bestow qualities of freedom on all conditions of life other than those specifically excluded. Does *any* social status short of actual slavedom really amount to *freedom*? Does life under *any* form of government which is not classically Nazi or Stalinist *necessarily constitute freedom*?

The clarity of this issue is somewhat hidden by the moral weight attached to these examples. Slavery itself has such a grave significance that it sometimes seems inappropriate to use it in order to discuss related conditions. Thus, to talk about sweatshop labour as a form of slavery, or to describe paid labour in general as "wage slavery", can be interpreted as lessening the importance of *real slavery*, such as that imposed on Africans exported to North America by European colonists.

Likewise, the Nazi regime is often discussed in a context outside its own reality. Because it presents such a clear-cut instance of totally unacceptable government, it is often cited to prompt people to think clearly about issues of morality and authority. For instance, when faced with the theoretical prospect of either obeying or resisting the state, the substitution of "Nazi" for "capitalist" can often reveal that behind an apparently moral objection to open-ended resistance *per se* lies an entirely contingent objection, based on the perceived legitimacy of the regime in question. The discussion, in this case, could then usefully be moved on, beyond the stumbling block of this illusory moral barrier, to an analysis of the legitimacy of other regimes and states, or indeed of states in general, to their inevitable use of violence to impose control, and then on to the ethics of defensive force against this violence.

But because the Nazi example is by far the strongest platform for this kind of discussion, it has been overused, thus weakening the impact of the comparison. Furthermore, like slavery, Nazism has scorched deep mental scars on humanity and it is often found offensive to *relativise* its historical reality by using it merely as a device to clarify the morality of our relationships with other kinds of states.

Unfortunately, the acceptance of Nazism as a unique affront to our freedom brings with it the corollary that *not-living-under-Nazism* is, in itself, seen as a kind of freedom, regardless of the conditions in any particular non-Nazi society in which we may live, in the same way that the horror of actual slavery brings with it the conclusion that *not-being-a-slave* is, in itself, a kind of freedom.

III

FREEDOM AS NEGATION

The underlying problem here is not with these specific examples, but with the way in which we are approaching the whole issue of freedom. We have tried to discover the meaning of freedom by looking at its absence, rather than its presence. We have taken as a starting point for freedom that which is in fact its ending-point. *Not-being-a-slave* is not a basis for freedom, but the bare minimum of what could remotely be termed "freedom" once the rest of our freedom has been taken away. It is the dregs of freedom, the last drop that is swallowed down anyway, even though it is too insignificant to quench any thirst.

The same applies to *not-being-in-prison* and to *not-living-in-a-totalitarian-state*. They have as much to do with the meaning of freedom as *being-in-a-coma-with-permanent-brain-damage* has to do with the meaning of being alive. Yes, *not-being-dead* is a kind of definition of being alive, but why frame it in such a negative way? Isn't death the condition of *not-being-alive*, rather than life being the condition of *not-being-dead*? Isn't *unfreedom* – the word should exist! – the condition of *not-being-free*, rather than freedom the condition of *not-being-unfree*?

The awkwardness of that last term, *not-being-unfree,* exposes the insecure foundation beneath all interpretation of freedom in terms of an absence of the contrary, an interpretation based on the negation of a negative. Being in prison is a *bad* thing; therefore not being in prison is a *good* thing. In making this statement, we are reducing life outside prison to the negation of *being-in-prison*. The condition of *being-in-prison* is taken as our starting point, and its opposite is bequeathed a narrow foundation on which nothing of any substance can be built. The idea of *not-being-in-prison* in no way evokes the infinite possibilities and richness of what life can involve if we are not holed up in a cell. Why would we even try to label life in terms of the absence of a constraint? Why not describe our current lives as *not-being-marooned-on-a-desert-island-surrounded-by-sharks*? Or *not-being-trapped-in-a-mountain-cave-by-an-irate-*

dragon? Why should the idea of sharks or a dragon even enter our minds in the first place, since they are in fact absent? Why would we seek out these random examples of a life-condition less full than our own in order to define what we have? In the same way, why would we seek out similar examples to try to define freedom? Why would we try to establish the meaning of freedom by reference to the absence of a prison cell, of a slave's chains or a literally-Nazi government?

IV

DIRECTION AND ORIGIN

An important issue here is the *direction* of our analysis. Our starting point is at the wrong end and by taking as that starting point the pathetic last remnants of freedom that we find in the conditions of *not-being-a-slave* or *not-being-in-prison*, we deny ourselves the possibility of reaching any other destination than that which can be reached from there.

Perhaps it is clearer to talk first of *dimension*. Any concept of freedom which can be drawn from the ideas of *not-being-a-slave* or *not-being-in-prison* is so thin as to be two-dimensional, whereas freedom itself is multi-faceted and multi-dimensional. The mode of *direction* stems from the fact that while it is easy enough to flatten a multi-dimensional concept into a two-dimensional one – albeit with serious impact on its substance and integrity – it is not so easy to expand a two-dimensional concept into a multi-dimensional one, particularly without any idea of what that multi-dimensional reality might look like or without any understanding of what the elements might be which would furnish the flattened version with the depth, breadth and substance of the complete phenomenon.

This question of *direction* is also leading us on to the idea of *origin*. The negatively-formed conception of freedom only gives life to freedom as the opposite of *unfreedom*. Freedom starts from the condition of *not-being-a-slave, not-being-in-prison* and so on. From that point, the idea can of course be expanded – there is probably nobody whose *entire* definition of freedom exists on such a low level. But the fact remains that the larger definition of freedom still depends on a mistaken assumption: that its origins actually lie in that artificial construct of being the opposite of *unfreedom*. The reason for this artificiality is obvious – the meaning of *unfreedom* is itself dependent on the meaning of freedom, which has not been established beyond this self-contained circle of definition. The whole idea is built on a vacuum. "Freedom is the opposite of the opposite of freedom" – a truism devoid of any real content.

It may be objected that the problem here is the use of the invented term *unfreedom* but this is merely convenient shorthand to help explain the general conception of freedom as absence of constraint, whether in the guise of prison bars, the Gestapo or an irate dragon. In fact, we can see that this same idea of *unfreedom*, which begins with *not-being-in-prison, not-being-a-slave* and so on and so forth, continues to be the bedrock of contemporary ideas of freedom as those are expanded in scope. Freedom *from* control, freedom *from* repression, freedom *from* restraint – these are all the *opposites of various kinds of unfreedom* and the key themes of what is termed our *liberty*.

V

FREEDOM AND LIBERTY

Although the word *liberty* means freedom, it lacks – in the English language – the same intensity. Perhaps because it has come to us from Roman civilization, via the Norman colonisation of England, it seems more remote than the raw authenticity we can sense in the term we inherited from the Old English *frēodom*. Moreover, there is no adjective related to *liberty* in English. We cannot be *liber*, only *liberated*, which is a secondary term applying to a specific process rather than a condition of being and furthermore implying a prior condition of not being *liber*. The idea of being *liberated* thus depends on that same negation, *unfreedom*, which we found to be the shaky foundation of our concept of freedom. Freedom, on the other hand, is the primal condition of being free – *frēo* in Old English, *frī* in Gothic and related to the ancient Sanskrit word *priya*, meaning dear. Freedom is *dear* to us all and means much more than the reduced, bureaucratic, *liberal* version implied in the term *liberty*, or worse still *liberties*, which sit so comfortably alongside the word *civil*, bearing all those associations with Roman law, the state, obedience, politeness, the denaturing of humanity into something containable within a *civil*ization.

The freedom of a *civil liberty* is secondary, relative, contained. There is always some smallprint to limit or restrict its scope. Indeed, implicit in its formulation is the potential for some kind of limit, referring as it does to an assumed relationship between state and *citizen*. And yet these *liberties* are often taken as being synonymous with freedom. Here is not the place to discuss the detail – it is the principle which is at stake. Freedom cannot be *based* on the privilege of *not* being subject to specific denials of freedom. It is true that we cannot be free if these freedoms are denied to us, but this does not logically also mean that if these freedoms are not denied to us, we are free! If I am liable to be burnt at the stake for declaring that the world is not flat, I am clearly not free as an individual. But the liberty to declare that the world is indeed round does not make me free. There is so much more to it than that. A whole series of these *liberties* still does not add up to freedom. An infinite number of these *liberties* does not add up to freedom, because they do not exist in the same conceptual dimension as freedom.

VI

FREEDOM-FROM AND *FREEDOM-TO*

One way to look at this is to draw a distinction between *freedom-from* and *freedom-to*. These concepts are related, but not in an equal manner. The first is totally dependent on the second for its substance. If I assert my desire for a *freedom-from* censorship, for example, I am claiming a *freedom-to* write what I want or for others to write what they want. If I claim a *freedom-from* random police stop-and-searches, it is because I believe people should have the *freedom-to* walk the streets without being intimidated by the state. The *freedom-to* is clearly implied by the *freedom-from* – the reason why I don't want to be censored is obviously because I want to write what I wish. Without the *freedom-to* lurking in the background, the *freedom-from* would have no meaning. What would be the sense in opposing police checks if I didn't support the freedom to walk the streets unmolested?

Such freedoms are indeed often expressed in their primary positive formulation. We demand the *freedom-to* self-expression, the *freedom-to* free association and so on. The *freedom-from* is recognised as ancillary to the *freedom-to*. However, this does not always happen and the *freedom-to* behind the *freedom-from* sometimes cannot be fully articulated. Let us go back to the example of prison. *Freedom-from-being-in-prison* means what exactly, in terms of a *freedom-to*? The temptation is to say something along the lines that it means the freedom to live how we wish to. But here again we meet the constraint implied by this negative formulation, the narrow foundations of its basis. To be free from prison is not *necessarily* to be free to live how we like. But in order to live how we like, we *do* have to be free from prison. The *freedom-from* is restricted – and restricting, if it is not relegated to its proper position as ancillary to the *freedom-to*. The underlying *freedom-to* has no such restrictions, which is why it has been described as multi-faceted and multi-dimensional and why it cannot be built from even an infinite number of *freedom-from* liberties. The freedom to live as we wish to, as we were meant to, as we could do. This is something vast, organic, complex and dynamic whose existence and scope simply cannot be derived from instances of its denial.

VII

FREEDOM AND WORK

The freedom to live how we wish to live is a fundamental freedom, and yet one which is not recognised by the inadequate code of *civil liberties*, drawn from the narrow concept of *freedom-from*. For example, there is no such thing, in the language of our society, as *freedom-from-the-need-to-work*. From this we may correctly deduce that there is therefore an *obligation* to accept the need to work. In fact, this is not so much an obligation as a compulsion. It may be dressed up as a *moral obligation* – a moral obligation to make an effort, to help perform tasks that need doing, to contribute to society and so on – but it is still a *compulsion*.

It suits the purposes of our unfree society to pretend that the idea of working is exactly the same as that of *working for someone else's profit,* to pretend that an unwillingness to be exploited is the same as an unwillingness to lift a finger.

It also suits its purposes to pretend that work is something necessarily performed in order to earn "money" – the tokens which are required for participation in its own functioning. *It therefore conflates an economic compulsion to participate in its structures with a "moral" obligation to contribute to the collective well-being.*

The natural efforts for survival made by all creatures – finding food, fashioning some kind of home or shelter – are not defined as "work". Work is seen as an economic, and thus purely human, activity. And any human whose contribution to society does not provide them with the appropriate tokens, or who lives outside the dominant economic reality, is not generally considered to be "working" at all.

When so-called "subsistence" living is derided by industrial society, it is not the lack of physical effort that is really being condemned, but the *lack of participation in its economic system* – participation of course amounting to *exploitation* for the overwhelming majority.

The emotional allure of simple ways of living remains strong even within the mindset of an industrial civilization, but this desire has to be projected on to socially-safe aspirations towards "dream" holidays or retirements. Meanwhile, there must remain the *economic obligation to participate in the system*, even though this may be presented as a moral obligation to work.

In our society there is, on the whole, a physical compulsion for the vast majority of the population to sell their labour for most days of the year and for most of their lives. Where people are able to escape that physical, economic, compulsion (by living on state benefits, perhaps), they are judged by dominant thinking to be guilty of infringing a moral code – but that so-called morality is secondary to the economic reality which has created the artificial "obligation" which they have avoided.

Our society can understand no such freedom as the *freedom-from-the-need-to-work* because the narrow base of a *freedom-from* cannot support the breadth of the question around labour. *Freedom-from-being-a-slave* is understood, but *freedom-from-having-to-sell-one's-labour-in-order -to-live* is not. The degree of compulsion involved in the latter is not considered sufficient to warrant the need for a *freedom-from*. The threat of destitution, misery, ill-health and starvation apparently does not undermine the kind of negatively-deduced freedom that takes as its foundation the idea of not being an actual slave in shackles, or of not being confined in a prison cell.

This perhaps results from the way in which the object of the *freedom-from* is not immediately obvious in a concrete way. It is not a specific employer who forces someone to work for them, nor is there a specific law which imposes the obligation to sell one's labour. If men and women were rounded up by riot police every morning and physically transported to factories, dockyards or call centres and made to work, the phenomenon would register on the level of *civil liberties* and the need for a *freedom-from* this compulsion would be registered in appropriate quarters. But so inadequate is the general understanding of freedom based on *unfreedom*, that the complexities of the real situation make the issue completely invisible to it.

VIII

FREEDOM AND LAND

Individual human beings are part of the life of the planet. Like all other living beings, they have to consume other parts of the living planet (such as fruit) in order to survive. The freedom to be able to so is thus a prerequisite for life. Food, such as fruit, has always grown on the planet and has always provided sustenance for humans and other creatures. Access to this food is as naturally a part of our existence as access to air. The freedom to live as other living elements of the planet live, and to consume the food produced by the planet, is so basic that one would think it hardly needed spelling out.

Here is another fact. Human beings are part of a living planet and, like most other living parts, live on the surface of the planet. Each one only needs a tiny part of the surface of the planet on which to lie down each night and rest. Depending on the climate, various levels of shelter are also needed for survival and good health. The freedom to exist on the surface of the planet is a prerequisite for human life. It is so basic that one would think it hardly needed spelling out.

The natural freedom to eat food and to have use of a human-sized space on the surface of the planet are denied us in contemporary society. At the root of this problem is the idea of land ownership. Long ago the land belonged to nobody. It doesn't matter exactly when, it's the fact that this was so that is important. Even if land-ownership was invented by the very earliest *homo sapiens* communities (which it wasn't) the fact would remain that prior to that there was no land ownership. The idea that individual human beings, with a lifespan of 70, 80 or 90 years, could claim to "own" sections of the surface of a four-billion-year-old planet is patently absurd. It is an idea that was alien to many non-Western cultures until the moment that Europeans produced bits of paper to prove that they were now the "owners" of what had hitherto been regarded as the flesh of Mother Earth.

All land ownership is therefore theft – theft not from an individual or specific group (which seems to be the only kind of theft recognised by contemporary society), but theft from the commons, from everyone. It is not just the historic taking of land into ownership which is theft, but the continued existence of that ownership. Pretty much every human being is born to find themselves, immediately, a victim of that renewed theft. There they are, a part of the planet, part of the life on the surface of the planet, and yet denied access to much of that surface.

This is not a theoretical theft, but a very *real* one with very *real* consequences. The land is not just an abstract area, but a life-support system. Food, such as fruit, grows there. There is material with which to build shelter, space in which to lie down at night and rest. The land is as much part of our lives as a river is for a fish, a tree for a bird, a cave for a bat. Take that away from us and we become "fish out of water" – helpless, homeless, hungry. This, of course, is where selling our labour comes in. Deprived of the freedom to live the way we are meant to, like the other creatures on the surface of the planet, we are forced to prostitute ourselves to the minority who stole the land from us in the first place. We supply them with our labour – always at a price less than the money they will make from it, otherwise they wouldn't bother – and they supply us with the means to *buy* temporary access to the things they have stolen from us, namely somewhere to live and something to eat.

Violence is deployed against us to impose this theft. Originally this would have come directly from the thieving individuals concerned, but now this has been codified and it is a *system* of violence and theft which oppresses us. The pieces of paper claiming "ownership" of parts of the planet are *legitimised* by laws, authorities and states. The violence used to maintain their theft is thus also *legitimised* and miraculously ceases to be violence. It is now upholding the law. Protecting order. Morality is reversed to the extent that anyone resisting the violence of the thieves is themselves regarded as a violent criminal. Over time, both the theft and the violence of the ruling criminal clique become invisible to many of the victims. They are taken for granted and their circular self-legitimisation is accepted at face value by those against whom they are deployed. The illusions (lies!) involved in this concealment add another layer on top of that of the original theft and the violence used to maintain it. *Most of those who are forced to sell their labour to survive have no idea that it is because they are the victims of a massive historical theft, still being renewed today for each new generation.*

Behind this issue lies the fundamental *freedom-to* which has been denied us. The freedom to live on the planet like other creatures do, and as our human ancestors did for a million years.

IX

LAW, VIOLENCE AND THEFT

When freedom is denied to us by the endlessly
self-reinforcing apparatus and assumptions of
authority, a key role is played by *laws*. Here the
freedom-from model of understanding freedom
runs into serious difficulties – *freedom-from-laws*
is certainly not a liberty readily recognised by
contemporary culture.

We can see behind this the way in which the
idea of freedom has been narrowed and lost. For
the ruling elite, general obedience to laws among
the population is necessary if the ongoing theft is
to be maintained. Disobedience is met with
violence (more theft, incarceration, officially
tolerated and encouraged physical assault) in
order that obedience is practised, even when not
believed in. For the management classes of our

society, it is also important that they *believe* in the importance of obedience to laws so that they may play their part in imposing them, and in imposing a belief in their essential rightness, on the population as a whole (including themselves!).

The *pretext* for the existence of laws, and their violent imposition on the population, is that they are needed for the good of us all. Without them, there would be chaos – all would be trying to rob or kill each other in a frenzy of greed and hatred. We are supposed to believe that this is true simply because the authorities tell us it is so. They can back up this claim with examples of despicable human behaviour, although inevitably these are drawn from *their* society, with its plethora of laws, rather from some imagined (and feared) society in which there are none. From this warped perspective inflicted on the population, the idea of a *freedom-from-laws* appears to have the same validity as a *freedom-from-gravity* or a *freedom-from-oxygen*. The concept only makes sense when it is transformed back into the positive from which the negative formulation of *freedom-from* is always drawn. The *freedom-to-run-your-own-life* or the *freedom-to-make-your-own-moral-judgements* already sounds more acceptable once any reference to laws has been removed. And why should laws be mentioned, even in their absence? They have been devised and imposed on human beings subsequent to our original conditions of existence (and, once more, it does not matter in the least *when exactly* they may have been inflicted on us – it is the principle of antecedence that matters here). The *freedom-to* which we cherish is the freedom to live naturally, as we are meant to, and not in the degraded condition of enforced dependence and obedience in which we currently find ourselves.

X

THE FEAR OF FREEDOM

The negative assumption behind the dominant attitude towards the *freedom-to-run-your-own-life* is that we are incapable of doing so. This belief has taken on many forms over the centuries, but it makes little difference whether one believes from "religious" conviction that human beings are born sinners or whether one's "scientific" view of the world sees an inherently brutal and selfish human nature, which renders us unable to arrange ourselves in a peaceful and constructive way.

Despite convincing counter-arguments which explain that co-operation and not competition is in fact the key to successful evolution, the negative view is still dominant today. Even those who argue that there is no such thing as human nature at all, and that everything about us is conditioned by our experienced cultural environment, are essentially adopting the same position. How can humans be expected to live naturally if we have no nature? How can we expect to survive without some kind of hierarchical structure if we have to be *taught* to be kind to each other, to co-exist in communities?

What is the meaning of a *freedom-to-live-as-we-wish* if we have a natural wish to do bad things, or if we have no natural wish to do anything at all?

It is this void created by the denial of the essential goodness of humanity that leads to the denial of our freedom. Freedom is regarded as something to be feared, rather than to be treasured or fought for. Limited, specific freedoms – civil liberties, *freedoms-from* – are tolerated because they are known, controllable factors. The idea of complete freedom, a *freedom-to-act-as-we-see-fit*, however, strikes dread into the heart of those with a negative or non-existent conception of human nature. Some might imagine dark, devilish forces being released from the uncontrolled human spirit – violent behaviour, selfishness, the domination of the weak, and the meek, by the strong and self-assertive. But why? Why should that be the case? Have we human beings so internalised the excuses for our enslavement offered by those who would rule us that we now believe them to be self-evidently true?

XI

NECESSARY GOODNESS

To believe that human nature is essentially bad
or to believe that there is no essential human
nature is necessarily to reject the idea that
human nature is essentially *good*. The latter
position is often dismissed as being naïve or in
some way religious in that it depends on a
certain *faith* in human nature. This is not the
case. The point is that humans – like other
creatures – *need* to co-operate with each other in
order to survive. The *goodness* involved in such
co-operation is therefore not of a saintly, other-
worldly kind which can be opposed to a more
pragmatic "human nature" geared towards
survival. It is, instead, a kind of *goodness* that is
altogether part of human nature and life itself. It
is the *goodness* not of any kind of artificial moral

code, but of things working as they *should*.

The misunderstanding of the idea of a goodness of human nature perhaps then relates as much to the idea of *goodness* as to the idea of *nature*. It might be objected that, according to this argument, the two notions are so interdependent for their definitions as to make any such statement meaningless. If *good* means *according to human nature* then this guarantees that human nature is *good*, without any regard to the content of that quality. If killing each other for no reason was part of human nature, then, it would seem, killing each other for no reason would be *good*.

This approach, however, ignores the fact that the *goodness* of human nature amounts to behaviour *necessary to ensure survival*. Killing each other for no reason could form no part of that: a species in which individuals were constantly murdering each other, or starving each other to death, would have died out hundreds of thousands of years ago. The point is that we are – indeed we *have to be* in the interests of our own survival – *social* beings. We are *innately* social beings with an *innate* interest in co-operation and mutual aid. As human beings, we are not social beings in the same way as, say, ants are social beings, or in the way that starlings or antelope are social beings. As humans, we have a degree of individual independence from group instinct which is unknown beyond the higher apes. *But the fact remains that we are innately social beings.*

If, then, we release a human being from all external restrictions and allow them the *freedom-to-act-as-they-see-fit,* we are not releasing them to behave in any random way. If we are truly released from *all external restrictions* there only one way in which we can behave – the way our inner nature dictates. If our nature is towards solidarity and mutual aid – because that is the way we have to be in order to survive – then that is the behaviour which will be released by our freedom.

Now, of course, people don't always act well. They can be brutal, greedy, selfish, manipulative, cruel and so on. But what is the context in which they have become this way? Are they free from all external restrictions? If they live in our contemporary "civilization", the answer will be a resounding "no". The behaviour of people living in the *unnatural* environment of contemporary society can tell us nothing about what their behaviour would *naturally* be. And yet this behaviour is cited in evidence to that effect. People behave like this *now,* so that must be how people will *always* behave, under *any* circumstances. *The dysfunctionality of human beings in contemporary society is thereby used as an argument to justify the continued existence of that same society!*

Imagine 200 songbirds kept caged in a tiny, enclosed area. Driven mad by the lack of freedom, the inability to fly more than a few flaps at a time, the constant competitive scrabbling for food and water, they would probably become ill-tempered and aggressive. Imagine a caring child imploring the keeper of the songbirds to set them all free, so that they might live happy, natural lives in the fields and woodlands. And now imagine the keeper explaining that it wasn't safe to let them out. See how aggressive they were! They would attack other birds, fight amongst themselves on a much bigger scale. And how would they manage to eat and drink without him to feed and water them every day? They had no idea of how to fend for themselves in the wild. As for any suggestion that they might have an innate ability to do so, an innate sense of how they might live outside of the nightmarish cage – well, that was utterly unprovable and, frankly, absurd.

To say that human beings are *innately good* is simply to say that human beings innately behave like human beings. This should come as no surprise! We feel able to describe this innately human behaviour as *good* because we, too, are human beings and such behaviour corresponds to our innate conceptions of *goodness* and *rightness*. Risking one's life to save a child from drowning in a river may be part of our innate co-operative behavioural tendencies because of the longer-term benefits to the wider community of a child's survival, but we don't need to rationalise it that way. We just know that it is a *good* thing to do. It is what we all hope we would do in the same circumstances.

If human behaviour were essentially bad, or neutral, we wouldn't have that automatic impulse, or automatic approval of others who act in that way. If we were really all just selfish individuals we would let the child drown – unless, perhaps, it was our own child or part of our own larger family, to which we had extended the scope of our individual selfishness-instinct. But our minds don't work that way – we have the impulse to try to save (or, at the very minimum, the feeling that we *should have* tried to save) any child. We might also, of course, have the same urge to save adults, or non-human animals, but the child example is particularly clear.

XII

RIGHT AND WRONG

While the innate goodness behind the desire to save someone is almost *instinctive* in its immediacy, there are other instances where we can see that the *idea* of *goodness* as a principle exists alongside the *manifestation* of goodness as an act.

This idea – of what is the *right* way to behave – is so deeply ingrained within us that we don't always realise it is there unless it is sparked into life by circumstance, particularly instances of people *not* behaving in the right way. We are capable, without any training or external code, of passing judgement on examples of human behaviour.

Suppose there is an island where the inhabitants have learnt they are all to be evicted

39

from their homes to make way for a nuclear weapons base. They also discover that the politician who agreed the deal has subsequently accepted a high-paying consultancy post with the nuclear arms industry. According to the external code of rules to which the islanders have been taught to refer, this politician has done nothing wrong – his conduct is entirely within the law. However, it is plain to everyone else that what he has done *is* wrong. Where did this alternative idea of right and wrong come from? Maybe it is part of the popular culture of the island and people have learnt it from each other. But why is it part of that popular culture? Why is this hypothetical response to a hypothetical situation *universally plausible*? Can we imagine a society where the people did *not* think this politician's actions were morally wrong?

It is also worth noting the *kind* of reaction which is prompted when somebody breaks our shared moral code. If the corrupt politician had merely infringed some written code of conduct, the focus would perhaps lie more in the detail of his transgression, on the evidence of his malconduct, the possible means of legal redress open to the community and so on. But when it is a matter of something plainly *wrong*, as in this case, the response is likely to be *anger*. Anger is a reaction that comes from a different place to that analytical part of the brain that might assess somebody's compliance or non-compliance with a set of artificial rules. It is an emotion that can often barely be contained or controlled by the conscious brain. It arises from the unconscious levels of our being – that very uncharted realm in which we might expect to find the innate moral code which has been broken.

A young unarmed protester, trying to climb a fence, is shot dead at point-blank range by armed police. They lie about what had happened, claim that he was killed by fellow protesters shooting at the police, plant molotov cocktails in his rucksack, circulate false stories via the media about his supposedly violent criminal past, forge emails and social media posts from him and others showing that they were in the pay of a sinister foreign power. But the plan backfires. All the details of the murder and the cover-up are eventually exposed. The reaction will undoubtedly be widespread *anger* at the way the police have acted, anger which is quite likely to take on a physical form. It is of no relevance at all that the authorities will eventually and inevitably clear the police of any serious wrong-doing – the idea of an *injustice* exists deep inside us all and we therefore recognise and respond to specific instances of injustice in a natural and untaught way, with an anger that swells up from the invisible core of our being, far beneath the layers of acquired cultural behaviour.

With both the above examples, the idea of moral right and wrong still arises from the innate survival-related need for co-operation in human communities – it involves the common good. Where that principle is betrayed, a *wrong* act is seen to have been committed. But this pragmatic explanation for humanity's functioning as a social organism does not devalue the morality involved or the concepts of good and bad, right or wrong. As human beings ourselves, these are *our* moral concepts too. Within the context of that subjectivity, the human subjectivity – which I can confidently declare embraces all those reading this text! – these moral judgements are not at all relative, but *absolute*. As humans conversing with other humans, we can safely work on the assumption that there *is* such a thing as *right* and *wrong* – even if we can ultimately appreciate that this is contained within our shared human subjectivity. Some cultural values differ between communities, of course, but the deepest human conceptions of right and wrong are innate and universal.

XIII

THE DESIRE FOR FREEDOM

There is a corollary to the fact that this innate sense of doing the right thing is not something that can be taught to us and is not something that we need to be ordered to do by laws. This is that if we are *prohibited* from doing the right thing by laws, we will be strongly tempted to *break* those laws – only the deterrence of violence, humiliation and incarceration offered by authority might dissuade us from doing so.

Here perhaps is the source of that *fear* of human nature that we mentioned above. It is the fear of those who would control humanity that there might be something stronger inside us than all the barriers (mental as well as physical) that they have erected around us to keep us in our place. *Their fear of human nature is a fear of*

freedom itself, a fear of our desire for freedom.
For the desire for freedom forms part of our
innate nature – it is a dimension which is
necessary in order to ensure that that innate
nature can be fully expressed. What use would be
an innate nature that failed to assert itself at the
first hint of some kind of difficulty or restriction?
What use would be an innate urge to save the
drowning child if it was thwarted by a riverside
noticeboard announcing that under council by-
laws it was forbidden to go into the water? What
use would be an innate dislike of corruption and
injustice if there was no naturally-generated
anger to translate that dislike into a physical
response? There has to be some kind of
propulsive force behind any facet of our nature in
order for it to consistently realise itself
regardless of external conditions.

To say that we are all born good, does not
mean that we will grow up to be good, because
our experience and cultural environment will
obviously affect our individual character and
behaviour. But it does mean that the goodness
remains inside us, an inner core of gold, even if it
is covered by layer upon layer of selfishness. And
the pro-active strength of human nature, its in-
built desire to realise its own freedom, means
that it will always be trying to reassert itself,
even if ultimately it does not succeed in doing so
in that particular individual. To deny this, to

deny the innate goodness (*human-ness!*) in each one of us, is to deny the essence of life itself.

XIV

INNATE CONCEPTS

We might ask what it means, on an individual psychological level, *not* to believe that humanity is essentially good? Even if this is a received opinion, would one not test it out on oneself? And what is happening inside someone who does just this and concludes that they themselves are not essentially good? Does not the fact that this judgement can even be made, suggest that there is *someone* deeper inside the individual who is closer to the idea of good, who is able to evaluate the outward behaviour of that person on the basis of an inner set of ethical values?

Likewise, what is going on when someone says it is "naïve" to believe that human nature is essentially good? Since the word "naïve" is related to the word "innate", is this itself an admission that the idea of goodness is something we are born with? If so, then presumably the assumption is that we subsequently learn from experience that this is not so, that people are *not* innately good? But how can we say we have learnt this, when all we actually encounter are people like ourselves, whose experiences in an unfree civilization have affected their behaviour and jaundiced their opinions? Our cynicism is mutually self-reinforcing. We are merely scowling at our reflection in the mirror and denying that there could ever be such a thing as a kind expression. Furthermore, the very fact of *denying* that there is an innate goodness of human nature still confirms the existence of the notion of *good*, even in this negative context. Where does this concept come from, particularly if we are claiming that *actual* goodness is hard to come by in the real world? The answer is that our concept of good, even in the context of denial, comes from *deep within ourselves*, from the same layer of self from which is issued moral judgement of our own personal behaviour and that of others. We all know what *good* means, even if we don't think it exists in ourselves or in others. And the fact that we know what it means proves that it exists – on an abstract level, of course, but that applies to the existence, rather than the application, of any such terms. The existence of a concept is not dependent on its application on a practical level. The concept of *three-ness*, for instance, exists in an entirely real, though abstract, way, without the need for there to physically be three of anything to which it is applied.

More than that, this abstract existence of goodness occurs *within the human mind*, within our minds, even within the minds which confirm its existence by way of denial of its innateness. By its very definition, good is not a neutral concept, but something to be aspired to, in the same way as *bad* is something to be avoided. Without that quality, it has no meaning or even existence. Simply by recognising the idea of goodness, we therefore necessarily recognise that we should *aspire* to act in a *good* way. Since the recognition of goodness as a concept is innate to the human mind, then so is the recognition of the moral obligation to aspire to be good.

What is the difference between an innate awareness of the existence and desirability of goodness and an innate *tendency to goodness*? Not a great deal. A tendency is only a tendency and none of us ever manages to be good all the time. An awareness of the desirability of goodness, and particularly the awareness that we are not fully living up to it, does in fact amount to a tendency to goodness – with a strong streak of self-criticism that can, in fact, only strengthen the tendency. Given that human goodness is a dynamic aspiration, a movement *towards* something rather than a completed state, this tendency to goodness is, in real terms, the same as human goodness itself. In other words, the thought that we personally are *not* good, and that humanity is *not* good, is an expression of a potential desire *to be* good and thus a recognition of the notion of goodness, a recognition of its desirability and, as such, a manifestation of goodness itself.

XV

ASSUMPTIONS OF AUTHORITY

We have seen that the notion of human goodness relates essentially to our social nature. Our concept of doing something *good* or *right* revolves around the idea of not acting selfishly, for our own narrow individual interests, but with others' welfare at heart. This impulse towards *goodness* is innate within each of us, not because we are pure or saintly in any way, but because this is how humans behave. This is how humans *have to* behave in order to survive as a species – not through the *badness* of ruthless competitivity but through the *goodness* of co-operation.

We have been taught to believe that there is no such thing as this innate goodness in our nature, no such thing as the natural tendency to mutual aid and solidarity. *This lie is essential if we are to submit to an authority which tells us we need it.* Authority says that there is no such thing as an innate human goodness and solidarity and that therefore we need laws, deterrents, punishments, police, courts, hierarchies, states and so on to keep everything in order. Complete freedom, a *freedom-to-live-how-we-wish*, is therefore out of the question. Indeed, says authority, we cannot even think of freedom in such general terms. Freedom is about specific *freedoms-from*: like the *freedom-not-to-be-in-prison* (which you can have if you obey the rules that authority says are necessary to keep humanity in order, in the absence of an innate sense of co-operative self-organisation!) or the *freedom-not-to-be-a-slave* (so long as you define slavery in the narrowest of historical terms and refute any equation with wage-slavery, which is the prevailing condition of most of humanity).

We see here a series of assumptions. The idea that we cannot have complete unrestricted freedom is based on the assumption that human beings cannot be *trusted* with that. The idea that we cannot be trusted is based on the assumption that there is no such thing as an innate tendency to goodness and co-operation. The idea that there is no innate tendency to goodness is based on the assumption that goodness is an *artificial construct* devoid of any practical content, rather than an inherent aspect of humanity's ability to survive. The idea that this innate goodness has nothing to do with survival is based on the assumption that humanity is merely a *collection of individuals*, with their own personal survival as a priority, rather than a *social organism* with collective survival as its aim.

Here we have come to a key point in our understanding of the difference between true, complete, freedom and the lesser freedom presented to us in contemporary civilization. The starting point for all the *freedoms-from*, the *civil liberties*, which are falsely presented to us as being the same as real freedom, is always the *individual* rather than the *social organism*.

XVI

COLLECTIVE FREEDOM

For the modern mind, the concept of *collective freedom* sounds like an oxymoron. There seems to be an opposition between an idea of freedom founded on the individual and a level of collectivity to which that individual must apparently in some way be subordinate. The solution to this apparent opposition is presented as a "balance". According to this view, freedom, conceived of in terms of the individual, has to be weighed against collective interests. The "balance" consists of restricting the freedom of the individual in the interests of a collective well-being. The two-dimensional formulation of where to "strike the balance" between the two extremes – individual interests and collective interests – is treated as the base line for political positioning on the issues surrounding freedom (or, in fact, the thinner entity of liberty). Libertarians will tend towards the individual-first end of this scale, whereas authoritarians – claiming a commitment to collective well-being – will tend towards the other. Others will hover around the middle, unsure as to what extent either should take precedence.

Needless to say, this way of looking at the issue is based on serious misunderstandings and creates whole new labyrinths of confusion for those who take it as their starting point. *At the heart of it is the error which we have already encountered, of regarding the individual as an entity solely concerned with him or herself, and without any innate sense of the need for social co-operation.*

It is only if one regards individual interests in this way, as being fundamentally in opposition to those of the collectivity, that one has to start thinking of how to restrict the freedom of the individual in order to protect the interests of the collectivity. Likewise, it is only if one regards the collectivity as fundamentally opposed to the freedom of the individual that one has to think in terms of restricting collective interests in relation to those of the individual.

The notion of an opposition between individual and collectivity, and the need to strike a "balance" between the two, necessarily involves a weakening of both, for misconceived reasons. *The truth of the matter is that individuality and collectivity are merely two aspects of the same thing. Individuals are innately social and form part of a social organism. That social organism, the collectivity, is itself composed of individuals.*

XVII

INDIVIDUAL AUTONOMY

Having already discussed the way in which the individual has an innately social aspect, we need to consider the role of the individual from the point of view of that social collectivity. Individuals are as necessary to a human collectivity as our limbs and organs are to our own individual bodies. Without them we would not even exist, let alone function. Regardless of this fact, we exist in our own terms as something more than the mere aggregation of a number of component parts.

In many ways individual humans appear *very different* from the limbs and organs of a body. We are not physically attached to anything else. We are able to choose how we behave. We are nothing like a person's ear, or kidney –

merely performing the physical function which we are shaped to perform. But the differences are more in terms of complexity than principle. If we accept that we, as individuals, are social creatures then ultimately we are carrying out a certain role on behalf of the collectivity.

The most fundamental role we play, as individuals, is in allowing the collectivity to *actually exist*. Without individuals, a human collectivity is not real. We are the manifestation, in real terms, in flesh, of the abstract entity of collectivity. We also enable the collectivity to *live* – not just to be, but to function, evolve, react, create and self-regulate. This is where the autonomy of the individual human comes in so useful for the collectivity – it provides a flexibility, a steering mechanism, a sensitive nervous system that would not exist if we were only able to act out inherited instinctive life-patterns.

It is important for the collectivity that individuals are free to live according to the subtlest demands of their nature, for only in that way can the collectivity also live according to the subtlest demands of *its* nature. The individual is part of the collectivity and the collectivity is made up of individuals. *They are the same living thing with the same interests at heart.*

A collectivity cannot be free unless the individuals who make it up are all free. An individual cannot be free unless they are living in a collectivity which is free, that is to say in which all individuals are free. There can be no such thing as a free individual in an unfree society.

The symbiotic relationship between individual and collective interests is perhaps hard to grasp for those who have learnt to see the concepts as fundamentally opposed. When we see a group of people, what do we see – the group or the people? The collectivity or the individuals who make it up? *If we cannot see both at exactly the same time, we can come close enough through a kind of oscillation.* As with a trick illustration which can show two completely different images, depending on how we look at it, we can flip instantly between seeing the group and seeing the people, the collective and the individual.

XVIII

FREEDOM IN RESPONSIBILITY

It is this ability to see both pictures, to embrace a paradox and transcend it with a higher level of understanding, that is entirely lost in a flattened way of thinking which sees only two-dimensional oppositions, for which the sole resolution is an unsatisfactory "mid-point" which excludes the vital content of each "side" of the issue.

Our transcendent point of view also reveals a previously unsuspected meaning for a much-abused word – *responsibility*. In the context of a fake opposition between the ideas of *collective* and *individual* and between the ideas of *collective* and *freedom*, *responsibility* is given a particular sense. It is used to describe a quality which must be adopted by the individual in the interests of the collectivity, but which will inevitably involve a certain loss of freedom.

This misunderstanding of the word can only arise from a false assumption. If the *freedom-to* sought by the individual is to live according to their nature, and if that nature is essentially *social*, then the assuming of responsibility for the wider collectivity need in no way involve a loss of that freedom. Indeed, the *contrary* is the case. The assuming of social responsibility is the fulfilment of the individual's freedom to act in accordance with human nature, to act as part of a living social organism. *Complete freedom is the same as complete responsibility, not its opposite!* To present responsibility as in conflict with freedom is therefore to reinforce the fake view of individual nature as inherently indifferent or even hostile to the collective good – it is to regard individual human beings as somehow unconnected to the species of which they indisputably form part.

Part of the confusion surrounding the term *responsibility* arises from the manner in which it is abused to suit certain purposes. It is often conflated with the notion of *conformity* or *obedience* not to the interests of the collectivity, but to an entity which is passing itself off as representing those interests (we will return to this issue later). There is said to be a *responsibility* to obey the law, for instance. This responsibility is not imagined as emerging from an individual's own judgement, based on innate concepts of right and wrong – hence the perceived *irresponsibility* of "taking the law into your own hands". Instead it is seen as being required in the interests of a collective good – but a collective good defined from above rather than below, separated from the natural notion of *goodness* (flowing, as we have seen, from the need for co-operation and survival) which forms part of a free human collectivity. It may be that the law in question (the prohibition of murder, for example) coincides with these considerations, but this amounts to no more than that – a coincidence, or a convenience, in that it reinforces the illusion that the law arises from considerations of collective good. The important point is that the responsibility in question is seen as something that must be accepted *regardless* of one's free conscience, rather than as the result of it.

XIX

REAL AND FAKE RESPONSIBILITY

There is an important conflict here between fake and real responsibility, between imposed and free responsibility, between responsibility dictated from the outside and responsibility assumed from the inside of the individual.

Ultimately, those who propose an imposed responsibility do so because they are afraid of the real responsibility which emerges from within. An *imposed* responsibility can be invoked to demand obedience to arbitrary rules constructed for the selfish interests of a minority which maintains control of stolen wealth through the violence of authority in all its forms. A *real* responsibility could well lead individuals, or communities, to challenge those arbitrary rules and the phoney morality built up around them.

Let us go back to the hypothetical community of islanders who are about to be evicted from their homes to make way for a nuclear weapons base. A protest march is staged against the plans, which is allowed to take place, under strict conditions, because, after all, the islanders have the *civil liberty* to voice their opinions within the law. However, at a key point in the route, the march suddenly veers away from the planned destination in a local park and heads for the home of the corrupt politician who approved the plans. In official terms, those involved in this diversion from the authorised route are immediately considered "irresponsible", particularly as a young protester is later shot dead by police while trying to climb a fence at the politician's home. Their *fake responsibility* to obey the rules set out by the authorities will always trump any *real responsibility* to do all they can to stop the community being evicted to make way for a nuclear weapons base. Their *fake* responsibility is at odds with their *freedom-to-act-as-they-see-fit* while their *real* responsibility arises from the assertion of that very same freedom.

This is why the contemporary concept of responsibility is seen as being in contradiction to freedom. Our society is not interested in the idea of people finding the freedom to accept responsibility, because if that responsibility is rooted in freedom it is dangerous to the whole system of self-legitimising falsity which has been built up to stifle the natural functioning of human communities.

Real freedom and real responsibility are so intertwined and interdependent in their meaning as to be almost inseparable. As well as needing the freedom to be authentically responsible, we need the responsibility to accept that freedom. When we talk about the freedom to be free we are also talking about the responsibility to accept responsibility. We need to be free to take on the responsibility of accepting our responsibility to be free – in other words, our minds must be sufficiently clear of selfishness for us to be able to accept the burden of understanding that we have a duty to the social organism to act as our innate nature tells us to. The two terms, freedom and responsibility, leap over each other and chase each other on into a self-deepening spiral of symbiosis.

XX

THE STATE VERSUS COLLECTIVITY

If people often wrongly regard the idea of a collectivity as being fundamentally opposed to individual freedom, it is no doubt because of the way the notion has been abused.

The problem arises when some artificial construct is held up as representing a human collectivity or even as *being* the human collectivity, although it is not formed and steered freely in the natural way. We are basically talking here about the state, an entity of any size (up to and including the potential existence of a global state) which is claimed by its supporters to enshrine the common interest of the human collectivity it embraces. It clearly does nothing of the sort – indeed, its real function is to suppress the organic freedom of the collectivity in favour of structures and strategies reflecting and defending its own interests. And what are its own interests? Even if we accept the idea of a theoretical state completely free of corruption by private agendas (which is in fact impossible, as we will see), the interests of the state are not identical with those of the collectivity. By virtue of its very existence, it sets itself, and its role, apart from that of the collectivity. Its recognition of itself as a legitimate representation of that collectivity, and its demand that those under its control also recognise that legitimacy, becomes, itself, its primary *raison d'être*. Taking as its starting-point the assumption that it is itself legitimate (as it must, if it is to exist) and a genuine incarnation of the collectivity, it immediately distances itself from the actual interests of the collectivity. In the eyes of the state, it *is* the collectivity, therefore the real collectivity, outside of the state, cannot exist! Worse than that, the real collectivity, when it manifests itself in some way, is not only unrecognised for what it is by the state, but regarded as an enemy of the state and a threat to its legitimacy. This is obviously true – the re-emergence of the real collectivity *does* represent a threat to the state. But the problem is that the state does not depict the situation in these terms, convinced as it must be that it itself is the incarnation of the real collectivity. Instead, it paints the emergence of the real collectivity in terms of a problem – disorder, subversion, instability and so on. The state's point of view, and its interests, therefore become still further divorced from those of the genuine collectivity.

If this point of view was only held by those controlling the state this would hardly matter, but unfortunately it tends to be much more widely shared. The claim that the state is the same as the real collectivity is a *lie* and as such its intention is to *deceive*. The victims of this deceit will often include people with a strong innate belief in collectivity, in the need for individuals to work together for the common good. Having been tricked into thinking that the state represents that collectivity, they project their commitment to collective well-being on to the state. From there onwards, it is a slippery slope. They accept that the state, in the interests of the common good, has to achieve some kind of "balance" with individual freedom (as that freedom can never be expressed through the blocked, above-down structures of a state). They accept that the state has a right, or even a duty, to repress manifestations of what is in fact genuine collectivity in order to protect the fake collective good that it purports to incarnate. They accept the state's conflation of *good* and *bad* with *legal* and *illegal*, accept its definition of *responsibility* as *obedience* to its laws. They accept the state's claim that its role is essential, that the idea of an innate human tendency to free co-operation is absurd and that human society would collapse into murderous chaos without the firm hand of the state in charge.

The motivation for this acceptance of the state's claims is essentially *well-meaning*, arising as it does from a sense of the importance of a collective level of human existence. But hand-in-hand with these good intentions, comes a fatal degree of gullibility. The whole system of *democracy* behind which the modern state hides itself is designed to retain the allegiance of such gullible individuals. The flimsiest and most transparent illusion of power somehow resting in the hands of the population seems to be enough to fool them. Perhaps, in truth, they *have* to believe that they live in a democracy so that they can continue to believe in the legitimacy of the state. They *have* to believe in the state because, in their minds, the state represents the collective level of human existence which they know is essential for the common good. From their perspective, not only is it *irresponsible* to fundamentally challenge the existence of the state but even *selfish* – for they can only see opposition to what they regard as a genuine incarnation of collectivity as stemming from anti-social individualism.

These people, these victims of the state's

self-justifying deceit, might therefore, on some level, feel obliged to internally censor, to block out, the knowledge that democracy is a sham, as the collapse of their faith in the legitimacy of the state would leave such a void in their understanding of the world.

XXI

THE CRIMINAL POWER OF THE STATE

It was necessary when examining the role of the state to take as a basis the theoretical idea of a state uncorrupted by private interests – only by doing this was it possible to clearly examine the inherent nature of a state without the complication of additional layers. However, the truth is that this theoretical model state has never existed and could never exist. To see why, we need to grasp why states come into existence in the first place. It is all about power. Not necessarily about the creation of power – for some kind of power must already have existed in order for a state to be created – but about the consolidation of power.

The state takes a raw physical power – such

as that wielded by armed thieves against their unarmed victims – and legitimises it. It turns land theft into land "ownership", turns the brutal demand to *"do what we say or else..."* into "justice", turns cowed obedience into "citizenship" and so on. As we have seen, it often successfully persuades much of the population of the legitimacy, desirability and necessity of its role in exercising this power.

What is easily forgotten, in the fog of confusion created by its own fraudulent self-definition, is that the state is a *device* to exercise power, rather than the *source* of that power itself. The origin of the power lies in those behind the theft of land and the resultant disempowerment and subjugation of the population. The role of the state is to hide the criminal nature of their theft, and power, and to protect these from being challenged by its victims. The whole purpose of the state therefore lies not in representing and defending the collective interest, as it claims, but in subduing and attacking the collective interest in the interest of a minority of criminals. It is therefore not so much *corrupted by* private interests as *composed of* private interests. It is hardly surprising, in the light of this, that there is a complete contrast between the real collective interest and the collective interest as presented by the state – it has always been fundamentally in conflict with the real collective interest, even *before* we start to take into account its need to justify its own existence by denying the existence of that real collectivity.

XXII

NATIONS AND THE DENIAL OF FREEDOM

Yet more confusion is created around collectivity by the idea of a *nation*. In many ways, of course, this is similar to the idea of the state and the two are frequently merged into the idea of a nation-state. But the concept of nation goes deeper than the state in its claim to legitimacy, as it purports to arise from a natural collectivity that is theoretically separate in its identity from the state. The plausibility of the idea of a nation arises from its definition as an extension of communal identity, reinforced by its own mythologising of a certain *national history*. It barely matters that these national myths are invariably fictitious or that nations themselves are relatively modern phenomena – the end result is a theoretical level of collectivity which persuades large numbers of people of its authenticity. In the same way that the state's disguise as *protector-of-the-common-good* persuades some well-meaning people of its necessity, so the nation's disguise as natural collectivity appeals on an instinctual level and can capture the loyalties of those with little interest in the structure of society.

Where the nation coincides with the state, as it so often does today, it provides a further level of reinforcement for the state's legitimacy, this time on an emotional level. If people somehow sense that there is more to collectivity than the dry structures of the state, the idea of nation provides them with a focus for that need. While the state addresses the people as "you", the nation talks in terms of "we".

In fact, the nation does *not* represent a genuine collectivity. It is an artifice, rather than a living entity. It is defined with borders and passports in a way that would not be possible if it were a living community, constantly shifting, absorbing, adapting, in the way that all organic entities do. It is a fake collectivity, which purports to group together people on the basis of its existence without them being linked in any other way or having any interests in common. If these people did constitute a collectivity, they would so *in spite* of the phoney idea of nation, rather than *because* of it. It is hollow collectivity, invented for the purposes of control and not arising from real living people with real living connections between them. It is a negative collectivity, based more on the "identity" of *not-being-foreign* than on any genuine sense of internal cohesion. The flags, the institutions, the armies, the national sports teams, the ceremonies, the officially-encouraged xenophobia and cultural arrogance – all of these are designed by states to strengthen their own power through the lie of the nation.

There are times and places where nationalism seems to be a force for freedom, in the context particularly of an anti-imperialist struggle. But this kind of freedom is very much a collective version of the *freedom-from* as discussed earlier. *Freedom-from-imperial-control* no more necessarily amounts to authentic collective freedom than *freedom-from-slavery* necessarily amounts to real individual freedom. The problem with nationalism is that the hidden *freedom-to* behind the negative construction of a *freedom-from* is intrinsically limited. Nationalism can only claim the freedom for people to act together on the level of "nation" – a concept which it defines itself and the scope of which is not generally open to challenge. The collectivity is therefore not free to form and shape itself as it sees fit – it is tied into this artificial construct. Similarly, the individuals within the collective are not free in that they are defined from the outside as primarily members of this very specific artificial collectivity. Real human belonging to collectivities is complicated and overlapping, but nationalism insists on a flattening-out of the organic reality in such a way as to coincide with its own false construct. Any sense of belonging to a collective entity other than the "nation" (such as to a smaller community within the borders of that nation, or overlapping its borders, or to a disparate cultural community without specific borders, and so on) is (rightly) perceived as a threat to the idea of *national identity*. The fact that this type of belonging is so fragile, so easily threatened by other connections of belonging, betrays its complete lack of organic authenticity.

The most obvious problem with nationalist anti-imperialist struggles is, of course, that the possibility of their success implies the eventual creation of a nation-state in which it is impossible for freedom to flourish. Despite its attempts to disguise its true functions, any such state always implicitly accepts that it is at the opposite end of the "scale" to individual freedom, in that limited two-dimensional way previously described. It demands that individuals *relinquish* some of their freedom in the interests of the collective good which it claims to represent – a genuine collectivity, by way of contrast, is the *fulfilment* of individual freedom on a shared level. As such, the state denies freedom. By further pretending that it actually champions freedom on a collective level (the "freedom of the nation", for instance) and by ostentatiously allowing certain narrowly-defined "rights" to individuals in the form of *civil liberties*, the state *hides this denial of freedom*. This hiding in fact itself amounts to an additional offence: the denial of an understanding that freedom is being denied *is in itself a denial of freedom*. If we can go on to grasp that its multi-layered tissue of falsity *also conceals the fact that this hiding of freedom-denial is taking place*, we can begin to see how effectively the state, along with the ancillary concept of nation, stifles the possibility of any understanding of real freedom.

XXIII

SOCIAL ORGANISMS

What are the collective *freedoms-to* that are being denied to us by the imposition of a state?

To answer this, we have to go back to the origins of its power in the theft of land from common use. A people living on the land enjoys a certain independence that is unknown to urban populations. Access to food is direct. People enjoy a certain relationship to nature and its rhythms, which are also the rhythms of their own lives. This relationship is included within a culture shared by those living in the same area. This collective culture is a living entity, as real and complex as the "personality" of an individual. The dynamic relationship between the individual and this organic collectivity guarantees our freedom to be ourselves on a level higher than the merely individual. It is an aspect of our belonging to a social organism.

When a community is dispossessed of the land, when the land is stolen from the common realm by the creeping institution of private property, it is not just its material independence which is stolen from it. It also loses that collective consciousness arising from the shared culture of people and place. It is this collective consciousness which enables it to act and live freely, in the same way that it is our individual consciousness that enables us to live our individual lives. *This shared level of consciousness essentially amounts to a living entity in its own right, though not contained within a single body in the way that an individual is.*

When the common culture is destroyed, when the community is dispersed, this living entity is killed. When all the members of the community are able to go together to live in some other place, the collective entity can survive. But it is still damaged, as it was formed by the specific relationship with the land enjoyed by the community in their original home. Different landscape, different climate, different wildlife – no two places in the world are exactly alike and uprooted cultures may not necessarily thrive in unfamiliar soil. In time, of course, new cultures, new collective consciousnesses, will take root and grow. But this is not possible in our civilization. No community is ever safe from the encroachment of private property and the associated confiscation, exploitation and destruction of the land.

Seen from the point of view of the natural collective human entity, the *freedom-to* which it has lost is nothing other than the *freedom-to-be*. The existence of a group of people in a certain place constitutes the *being* of this entity. The flowering of a specific culture from that people and that place constitutes its *living*. The collective consciousness associated with that culture is its *thinking*. When the collective entity loses its *freedom-to-be*, all the individuals who were potentially part of it lose their *freedom-to-belong*. Since humans are *social* beings, for whom belonging is essential to their survival, these individuals are losing more than some superfluous and abstract freedom. They are losing the fundamental freedom to be the way they were meant to be, to be the way they have to be if they are to be *fully human* and to realise all the potential within them. We are so used to seeing humankind as consisting exclusively of individuals that we see potential as something strictly limited to the individual sphere. We imagine that an individual human can realise their full potential in splendid isolation. *But because we are social beings, and meant to form part of a social organism, we cannot fully become our true selves either in literal isolation or in the effective isolation of a society constructed on the basis that it consists of individuals and that the only form of collective existence that can exist is that created by the state.*

XXIV

COLLECTIVE CULTURE

The freedom to be part of a living culture is therefore not a secondary freedom, but a primary one relating to the completeness of the individual. As we saw earlier, the relationship between individual and collectivity is symbiotic: each needs the other. While the individual finds true self-realisation through belonging to a collective culture, the collective culture can only realise itself through individuals. Hence, perhaps, comes the sense of *purpose* felt by an individual contributing to a culture in some way.

The two kinds of realisation feed from each other, mutually deepening each other's validity. The collective culture *becomes real* by being expressed (in part) through an individual and the individual *becomes real* by acting as an expression of the collective culture. The feeling of making the collective culture real adds to the satisfaction felt by the individual, and the weight of this awareness makes the act of expression still more significant and the collective culture thus still more real.

Contemporary society offers no room either for the individual's freedom to be part of collective culture or for the collective culture's freedom to express itself through individuals. There is no room, in fact, even for the idea that a collective culture could be a real living entity.

There is more to culture than simply art, music, literature, dance, poetry, theatre, sculpture and so on, important though these all are. Culture, in the broader sense, could be used to describe the realisation of the collective consciousness. It is the *mind of the social organism*, manifesting itself in comprehensible forms through individuals' self-expression (the self, as expressed, being larger than that of the individual).

The idea of a social organism having a mind is so alien to dominant contemporary conceptions that it is worth reinforcing the basis on which it can be seen to exist. Individuals do not live in isolation, but (collectively) depend for their survival on the existence of co-operation and mutual aid within a larger supra-individual entity. That level of an organic collective entity is not as fixed or obviously coherent in form as that of the individual, but it nevertheless does exist in healthy human societies. While the physical presence of the collectivity may be seen as being made up of a certain number of individual human beings, its real coherence and importance lies on the intangible level of the shared culture, a collective consciousness enjoying a symbiotic relationship with the individual consciousness. Without this element of consciousness, this *mind*, the collective level could not even be seen as existing – a mere collection of individuals pursuing their own individual interests does not constitute a collective entity.

XXV

THE COLLECTIVE MIND

The mind of any organism is obviously of great importance. It is the mind of an entity that is aware of its own existence. It is the mind that assesses situations, makes decisions, steers it in a certain direction, weighs up the *rights* and *wrongs* of a given situation. This last point is crucial – for the innate sense of right and wrong, good and bad, which we find in the human individual, can also be found in the collective human entity. This has to be the case, for it is from the collective need for survival, from the collective nature of humanity, that the individual draws this sense. The presence of this sense of right and wrong within the individuals composing the collective entity means that it also exists on the less definable plane of collective awareness.

It is because the collective mind is able to make judgements about what is right and wrong that it is able to steer the course of the collective entity. The shared level of awareness is enhanced by the input of individuals within the collectivity, who are endowed with a degree of independence and unpredictability that releases the collectivity from the obligation to follow a fixed, or purely instinctive, path and provides it with flexibility, adaptability and creativity. The interreactions between individuals and collectivity, collectivity and individuals, will be too complex to be mapped out, embracing every kind of social and cultural relationship and participation within the group. *A multi-faceted, multi-layered, multi-dimensional, inter-responsive, infinitely subtle organic process will be taking place – the workings of a living mind.*

This is the *freedom-to-determine-its-own-fate* which must be enjoyed by every human collectivity in order for it to be considered free. This freedom is based on the existence of a collective culture, or mind, and further involves this mind being able to determine the life-course of the collectivity.

We have already seen that the separation of human communities from the land, and the denial of the existence of social organisms, risk destroying the collective culture at the heart of this freedom. There may exist no collective mind *capable* of directing whatever form of physical collectivity remains.

One of the most serious ways in which this mind can be blocked from functioning properly is when a large part of the population is cut off from it workings. Historically, this has been particularly evident in the exclusion of women from both formal and informal decision-making processes. It is possible that this exclusion has taken place as a result of the general dysfunctioning of the organic entity. Instead of flowing naturally, *power-from-within* is fixed into more rigid structures which are then dominated by those who set them up – or, more significantly, by the *way of thinking* that set them up. This then creates a vicious cycle in which participation in the decision-making processes is increasingly restricted to those prepared to take part in a pre-conceived manner and on the basis of certain hidden assumptions, including those that led to the separation of decision-making from the organic collectivity.

For instance, it might be assumed that certain social roles (such as those often performed by males) are of greater value than others (such as those often performed by females). These assumptions, being assumptions, are never challenged, but underlie the way various issues are regarded and handled.

Females might therefore be faced with the choice of participating in the processes anyway – and thus implicitly accepting these assumptions – or of deciding not to participate, thus reinforcing their own exclusion from the processes. It is because of the depth of the social assumptions made that the more recent re-inclusion of females into the structures of decision-making in the Western world has not redressed the problem – the damage has already been done. The structures themselves, and the assumptions they represent, are the blockage to the proper functioning of the social organism, regardless of the range of participants. Indeed, by emphasising the enhancement of its fake democracy by the inclusion of women, the dominant system attempts to bolster its legitimacy in the eyes of the female part of the population – the "right" to vote being a privilege other women had fought hard to "earn" and thus not something to be challenged by a broader understanding of the falsity of the "democratic" processes.

It is not inconceivable that this gender-exclusion is even the *cause* of much of the original dysfunctionality, rather than the result. Certainly any living being whose mind has been semi-paralysed is likely to behave, at the very least, in a slightly strange way. Were the original land-theft and the subsequent layers of self-justifying authority imposed on humanity, *made possible by a crippled collective mental state born of the domination of one gender by the other*? The suggestion cannot be readily dismissed and, though this issue is not the central theme of this text, it is worth emphasising that *no human collectivity can be termed free unless all the members of that collectivity are free.* That freedom includes the individual freedom to behave, and participate, in the way that they wish to and not to be restricted or defined by gender-related external assumptions. The idea of a *natural* functioning of the social organism should in no way be understood to involve *fixed* ideas of human nature based on gender, sexuality or any other such factors. On the contrary, the very notion of something being *natural* involves a depth of complexity and subtlety unimagined by any artificially-produced code or description of behaviour or personality. It is the *infinite variety* in their nature that allows human individuals to shape the collectivity in such a sophisticated and flexible fashion. Attempts to impose rigid identities or social roles on individuals thus disable the healthy functioning of the organism, whose life-flow depends on the freedom of individuals to contribute to the collectivity on the basis of their own inner motivation.

XXVI

REAL AND FAKE DEMOCRACY

There is a further barrier in the way of this free functioning of human society inasmuch as the state, as we have seen, refuses to acknowledge the validity of any form of collectivity other than its own and thus refuses to acknowledge the validity of any form of self-determination arising from such a collectivity.

A state which was open about its monopoly on power would thus clearly be seen to be denying a population the *freedom-to-determine-its-own-fate*. But contemporary states are not open about this and hide the reality behind the illusion of *democracy*. It has already been stated that democracy is a sham, but the reasons for this are now perhaps clearer. A genuine democracy, self-rule by the people, would arise from a free collective culture and would involve a free, organic, participative process of collective decision-making. Fake democracy, of the kind we know today, is an outright attack on genuine democracy. It removes all participation in the process and divides the community into a collection of separated individuals, each supposedly pursuing their own self-interest by choosing between a limited range of "representatives" aligned to various factions within the dominant system. The structure of the system blocks input on specific issues and indeed cuts out collective public involvement well before the point at which "issues" are even formulated – there is no opportunity to have a say in setting the agenda, let alone in challenging the form of the decision-making, the existence of the decision-making apparatus or the power of the state which it reinforces.

The subtle collective assessment of what is right or wrong, good or bad, what constitutes justice or injustice, responsibility or irresponsibility – informed by the deepest shared conceptions of the human mind, as well as by all the particularities of that specific culture – is replaced by a structure guaranteed to defend state interests, which are inherently at odds with the common good.

The state cannot acknowledge the idea of genuine democracy any more than it can acknowledge the idea of genuine human collectivities. To do so would be to relinquish the legitimisation of its monopoly of power which is its very *raison d'être*. All real freedom is anathema to the state.

XXVII

THE REALITY OF NATURE

If we are to understand what freedom means, and can mean, for human beings, we first need to understand what human beings are. Individual human beings are part of the human species. The human species is part of life on Earth as a whole. The Earth and everything on it is part of a living, interacting universe. This is not opinion, but fact. Life on the planet as a whole is referred to as nature. Humankind is part of that nature. This is not wishful thinking, or romanticism, but reality.

When we talk about the *freedom-to* be something, we can only ever mean the *freedom-to* be something that we already are or have the *potential* to be. It makes no sense, for instance, for me to talk about my freedom to be a horse. I can never be a horse, nor I can reasonably demand the freedom to be one. I may have a *desire* to be a horse, but that is something different.

The same applies to *freedoms-from*. It makes no sense for me to demand *freedom-from* the need to breathe air. It is part of my physical reality that I do have this need. Likewise, it is pointless to express the desire to be *free-from-nature*. We simply *are* part of nature, like it or not. We may express the *desire* to be set free from the perceived constraints of nature, but that is something different.

If people do have a desire to free themselves from "nature", or the "natural order of things", it is perhaps because these terms have been misused. They are often deployed to defend an existing way of organising society, or the way in which certain people think that society *should* be organised. This is merely the use of words to justify a certain stance – declaring this or that kind of behaviour to be "unnatural" for example – which has nothing to do with nature itself.

There is also a degree of suspicion around the idea of "nature" which results from the occasional over-romanticisation of the idea within our culture – itself no doubt a reaction against the denigration of nature in industrial society. This creates the impression that there is something naïve about any talk of living in harmony with nature, that this is a rather simple-minded notion based on a fundamental lack of understanding of reality. But this over-romanticised vision of nature is one that is frequently promoted by *critics* of the idea of *living-in-nature*, albeit in a negative way. They have projected an image of an imagined nature, which they know to be unreal, on to the understanding of nature held by others and dismissed that understanding on the basis of this false content that they have themselves introduced!

In fact, there is nothing unreal at all about nature. It is, itself, reality. It is *our* reality, as we are intrinsically part of nature. It is in the *denial* of our belonging to nature that the unreality resides. Our freedom too, our *real* freedom, can only arise from the reality of nature. We cannot be free *from being part of nature* – that is physically impossible. Instead, we should be looking at how we can be fully free *to be part of nature.*

XXVIII

THE FREEDOM TO BE REAL

Before we started to be excluded from the land, we enjoyed a *freedom* to live as part of the fauna of the planet. We enjoyed a relationship with the land that answered our needs as human beings, enabling us to live *freely* according to our own natures. This does not mean that life was perfect, or that life could ever be perfect. Human beings are flawed in the same way that all nature is flawed. But at the same time the beauty of nature includes these flaws, even depends on them. The flaws form part of reality, natural reality, and so do not strike us as being ugly. A withered branch, a tangled vine, a crumbling bank – these do not detract from the beauty of nature, but enhance it. The same applies to products of human labour. A medieval stone farmhouse with bulging walls, sagging roof and decaying window frames is not ugly. In fact, its imperfection is beautiful. Its imperfection is itself a kind of perfection, without any need for a certain regularity and smoothness with which we have come to associate that term.

Such is also the case for humanity itself. We are not perfect in the sense that a computer or a robot might be perfect. We all make mistakes, misjudge situations, behave in ways that we later regret. That is what being human is all about. That is what makes humanity beautiful, what makes life beautiful. It is our freedom to be ourselves, with all our flaws, that constitutes our humanity. So the idea of a human existence within nature should not be confused with any *unreal* conception of what this way of life might be like. It is the *reality* of a life connected to the land which constitutes its beauty. Moreover, immersion in that complex, subtle reality constitutes freedom.

Contemporary culture sets the idea of nature apart from humanity. It is treated as something to be treasured maybe (at the same time as being *mastered...*), something to be protected, looked-at and visited (at the same time as being *exploited...*), but always as a thing, or a collection of things, which does not *include* humanity.

We cannot stop being part of nature, because

that is our reality, but we can cease to *realise* that we are part of nature. This results in a gap, a discrepancy, between reality and our understanding of reality. Any such gap is dangerous, because our decision-making – individually and collectively – is not based on a true understanding of reality.

This is plain to see with regards to the direction human civilization has taken. Non-human beings are treated as objects. The living structure of nature – the reality in which we exist – is regarded as an impediment to human interests and is ripped up, torn apart and destroyed. Like a man perched high up in a tree, sawing off the very branch on which he is sitting, we have lost sight of our own reality, with disastrous consequences. *When we destroy nature, we destroy ourselves. We destroy our own freedom, too, because that freedom emerges from and depends on that nature of which we are part.*

What sort of freedom could there be for humanity if the surface of our planet became uninhabitable? To be "free from nature" – which is the motivating desire behind the delusion of industrial "progress" – is to be free from reality and, ultimately and logically, to be free from existence, from life. For a species which is biologically part of nature, to be free from nature simply equals death.

XXIX

THE LOSS OF BELONGING

We see this same gap between reality and our perception of reality in the relationship between individual and collectivity. It is an obvious fact that every individual human is part of the human species, and yet that truth is one that is so often obscured, on more than one level. The lie of national or racial "identity", for instance, promotes that entirely artificial and indefinable construct of collective belonging to a greater level of importance than that of the very real and definable human species.

Individuals, too, have little sense of being part of a greater organism. Yes, we all know that we are human beings but that often amounts to little more than a label of classification, in the same way that a chair can be described as being "furniture". We may have little sense of *belonging* to the human species in a very real, physical, organic sense – of being, as an individual, no more than a temporary and particular outgrowth of the enormous and complicated organism we know as humankind. In our culture our lives are presented primarily as *individual lives*. Our interests, our needs, our desires and, indeed, our freedoms, are presented in terms of the individual – except where the demands of false collectivities such as nations are expected to take precedence.

We cannot see that although we do indeed, as individuals, possess specific attributes of our own and a vitally important ability to act independently, all of that individuality *is still contained within a broader context of biological belonging*. This breaking-down of our self-awareness leads to the breaking-down of the health of the overlapping and concentric organisms of which we form part. The broader interests of the community, the human species or the living planet, are disregarded in the delusion that the significance of existence lies on a purely individual level.

XXX

BLOCKAGES TO AWARENESS

Throughout this text, freedom has been regarded as something that flows, or should flow, naturally. It is not something that has to be invented or erected in an artificial manner. Restrictions to that flow of freedom therefore appear in the form of various *blockages*.

On a physical level, there are already many blockages to our freedom – the theft of land, the inherent violence of authority and so on. We have now encountered the existence of blockages on a more abstract level – blockages to our consciousness or awareness. As individuals we remain part of collective entities, but our awareness of this is blocked. We, and those collective entities, all form part of a living organism called the human species, but our awareness of this is also often blocked. Humankind is itself a living part of nature on this planet and yet our consciousness of that has been lost to such an extent that it threatens to lead to our extinction, as well as that of the planetary organism of which we form part.

These blockages are *deliberately* created, not by individuals, but by the system in question. They are created as part of a wider process and are necessary to that process. If communities are to be disempowered so that their land and their labour can be exploited, it is essential that their sense of cohesion be undermined. The culture associated with that disempowerment and dispossession will therefore necessarily carry with it ways of thinking that encourage individuals to see the world only in terms of their *individual* interests and not in terms of communal interests. So, for instance, there might emerge a religion based on the prospect of the salvation of *individual* souls. Or a social theory in which evolution is shaped by competition rather than by co-operation – by the survival of the fittest (and also perhaps the most ruthless, the most selfish?) *individuals*. Or there may develop a code of social hierarchy or self-esteem based on *individual* status or wealth, where standing in the community is not defined by contribution to the community but by material success in relation to, and at the expense of, other *individuals* in the community.

These ideas will necessarily develop alongside the social phenomena they serve to justify and reinforce. Ideas which were previously widely held, with an emphasis on communal rather than individual identity, will increasingly be regarded as *old-fashioned* and restrictive. The idea of freedom will be redefined so as to represent the individualism of contemporary society. *It is important that any other way of thinking is not only displaced, but is eventually regarded as entirely undesirable and, ultimately, unthinkable.* This kind of blockage is a stage beyond a mere blockage of awareness. It is no longer simply a matter of an understanding that has been forgotten. Instead the understanding has been buried underneath several layers of assumption that make it impossible for the loss of understanding to be grasped, let alone corrected. Further blockages are created by the process to conceal and protect the original blockage. It is as if a disease which has gripped the human mind has managed to disable our immune system, leaving us unable to fight it off.

These blockages can be seen at every level. Along with the collective act of destroying nature must necessarily come a collective delusion that it is fine to do so. Therefore, the processes which involve the destruction of nature throw up ideologies that justify the destruction. "Nature was created for humankind to exploit. Human life consists of a struggle *against* nature, of which it is not really part. Nature is essentially brutal – red in tooth and claw – and humanity's assaults on it are therefore positive. We are improving the world around us, not destroying it. Humanity is the crowning glory of nature and therefore its own interests outweigh those of any other life-forms with whom we share the planet. There is an inevitable phenomenon called Progress in which parts of nature must unfortunately be sacrificed in order that we might continue on this ever-upward path towards future glories". All of these delusions contribute to a climate of thought in which humanity's *non-belonging* to nature seems self-evident and in which humanity is seen as having not just a right but a duty to dispose of nature as it sees fit for "its" own purposes (in truth, of course, the interests of the dominant elite).

XXXI

LAYERS OF MISUNDERSTANDING

As these assumptions take hold of the human consciousness, and the gap between reality and reality-awareness widens dangerously, further layers of blockage are laid on by the process.

One such layer might come in the form of an apparently critical analysis of society which in fact ignores some fundamental realities about the dominant system, or about human nature. This analysis is itself a blockage and plays its role of *protecting* the system from potential attack by *filling the space* which should have been occupied by a genuine philosophy of resistance and by luring would-be revolutionaries into the dead-end of its inadequate theorising.

Other layers clog up our understanding of the world in a myriad of ways, creating a fog of confusion in which any real clarity of thinking is impossible. Any intellectual challenge to the delusions of separation (*individual-from-community* or *humanity-from-nature*) becomes increasingly difficult, because the terms of discussion are no longer understood. If someone regards the idea of freedom as applying only to individuals, then the notion of a collective level of freedom comes across as nonsense. Worse than that, perhaps it will be conflated with the fake collectivity of "state" and "nation" and the idea dismissed on that basis. If someone has always assumed that nature is essentially brutal, then to talk of humanity's need to be fully part of nature is akin to suggesting that humanity *should be* brutal. If someone does not understand that "progress" is a specific socio-economic journey on which humanity happens to have embarked, rather than an historically inevitable trajectory, then to challenge its continuation seems to amount to the same thing as challenging the passing of time itself – "you can't turn the clock back!" If someone accepts that the process of industrial capitalist development is the *remedy* for poverty, misery, disease, and ignorance – rather than the cause – then anyone *opposing* industrial capitalist development is little less than a monster. If someone has always accepted the idea that narrow "rights" granted by the state amount to a *gift* of freedom rather than the implicit confirmation of a far larger *theft* of freedom, then they will not understand why freedom and the existence of a state are entirely incompatible. When the word "freedom" has been defined by the system/process to describe *the-way-we-live-and-think-today*, it is inconceivable that *the-way-we-live-and-think-today* could in fact be the complete denial of authentic freedom.

To strip away all these layers of misunderstanding we need to keep pace with them, or indeed a step ahead, by means of our own awareness of what is happening.

In order to regain our awareness of human belonging – our real physical belonging to real physical collective entities – we need to understand the significance both of that belonging and of our awareness of that belonging.

We need to be aware of the ways in which our awareness and our understanding are both blocked – so that we can find ways of removing the blockages. We need to understand why it is important for the system/process that they are blocked, why it inevitably generates thought-systems of a kind that will block them.

This understanding will tell us why, from our point of view, it is important for them to be unblocked. We will therefore be aware not just of the importance of the belonging *per se*, but of the importance of maintaining awareness and understanding of that belonging in order to prevent our natural freedom from being blocked. Where awareness and understanding are already blocked, and along with them our freedom, this understanding will point us towards the need to unblock them.

XXXII

DYNAMIC FREEDOM

Through identifying the fact that our awareness is blocked, and identifying the reasons for this and the need for remedial action, we are propelled from a passive position of *awareness-of-belonging* into an active stance of *reasserting-awareness-of-belonging*. In doing so, we are making an important step in terms of our freedom. Instead of merely being something we had, or something we lost, freedom is now something we are reclaiming and we are thus ascribing to it a new kind of value. Freedom no longer describes how things are, or were, but how thing *should* be. It is something that we *ought* to have.

We can immediately see that this is no longer entirely the same kind of freedom. It is a sort of second-generation freedom, a kind of freedom that has only come into existence because of the loss of the original freedom. Although its final aim is the regaining of that original freedom, it itself has taken on a new aspect, a dynamic aspect. There is a moral urgency behind it: it includes within itself the need for its own restoration (or rather for the restoration of the original freedom, which could not have included that dynamic aspect). This new kind of freedom also carries within it the idea of *change*, because without that it cannot realise itself. It is a freedom that incorporates the need to *dismantle the blockages* placed in the path of its original flow and acknowledges that there will be opposition to their dismantling and that this opposition will have to be countered. We are thus extending our idea of freedom to include the need to *fight* to restore the original version.

This is a necessary evolution, in the face of adversity. As we have seen, without the element of propulsion behind innate human tendencies they would have no way of asserting themselves to surmount the slightest difficulty. The fighting element must always latently exist in order to give our natural desires the vital strength necessary to realise themselves. It is the *life force* within each of us as individuals that is reasserting itself when we stand up to external pressures and insist on doing what we know is *right* and, as a result, insist on our *freedom to be able to do what is right*. Likewise, it is the life force within the collective human entity which inspires the understanding that we must be collectively free to do what is right and which inspires the struggle for that freedom.

There is, however, a danger here – namely, that this *fighting* dimension comes to obscure the original sense of freedom. So much fighting goes on, so many new ways are devised by authority to thwart these efforts, that the focus is entirely on the fighting and the issues around it. The understanding of freedom degenerates into one built entirely around the struggle and with only the vaguest idea of the nature of the original freedom for which people were fighting. Unrooted, it becomes prone to be swept away and lost in the first storm of adverse circumstance.

It is important to bear in mind that the scope of freedom itself is necessarily, logically, broader than the more specific need or urge to protect or restore that freedom. The freedom to fight for freedom is ultimately a secondary freedom, although a necessary one. *We cannot reach our destination without a journey, but that does not mean that the journey becomes the aim in itself.*

To grasp the meaning of real freedom we need to leave behind, for a moment, the contingent realm of practical or political freedom and consider its basis on the metaphysical plane.

XXXIII

METAPHYSICAL REALITY

We have addressed the need for an awareness of human belonging both to collectivities and to nature as a whole, and the fact that this awareness has been blocked as part of the process of the development of contemporary society.

There is a further layer to this phenomenon which now needs to be examined – the belonging of human beings to the universe. To appreciate the significance of this reality, we need clarity as to the way in which the word *belonging* is being used. When we say that the individual *belongs* to the collectivity, we are saying that he or she *is* an aspect of the collectivity. We cannot simply declare that the individual and the collectivity are the *same thing*, because the collectivity is obviously much larger than the individual. But while the nature of the collectivity consists of much more than merely that particular individual, the nature of the individual consists *entirely* of stuff that forms part of the collectivity. A fish consists of much more than just a tail, but its tail consists *entirely* of fish.

The same applies to the level of humankind. Humanity is a lot more than just me, but I am *nothing other than* human. I am one tiny part of humanity as a whole. A tree is a lot more than a twig, but the twig is *nothing other than* tree. It is a tiny part of the tree as a whole. The tail *is* the fish and the twig *is* the tree, but at the same time the fish is not *just* the tail and the tree is not *just* the twig.

Being entirely human also means I am entirely composed of that which makes up humanity. I am entirely of the planet Earth and entirely of the universe. It is easy to understand how this applies to physical reality. We all consist of the stuff that makes the universe and we are all contained within the universe. We *are* the universe, with the same proviso that the universe is a lot more than *just* us.

Things become more complex when we extend our definition of the universe beyond the purely physical. We are perhaps used to thinking of the universe as something that can only exist in physical terms, but its theoretical extension cannot logically be avoided. The moment we define something we put borders around it – so what lies *beyond* the borders that go around the physical universe? Alternatively, we might ask what was there *before* the physical universe existed. In either case, we are looking for something which is *not* existence itself but which necessarily allows and contains the *possibility of existence.*

But this entity, too, in order for us to be able to define it in our imagination, also has borders – and thus also has something beyond itself against which it defines itself. This yet-broader entity might be the *potential* for there to be a condition in which the possibility of existence is contained. Existence itself is, of course, also contained *within* this broader entity (as in the previous one), but as a "potential-level" entity it consists of much more than that. As well as existence, it also contains non-existence, the possibility of existence, the possibility of non-existence, the potential for a condition containing the possibility of existence or non-existence and also the potential for a condition that does not contain the possibility of existence or non-existence.

If we can describe that entity, then there must in turn be something higher, wider, deeper, than that beyond its borders – another theoretical bubble containing, in turn, all the smaller bubbles. And if we can say what that is, then it too must be definable in terms of what it is not, in terms of what lies even further beyond the concept it incorporates. Theoretically, there could be an infinite number of such ever-expanding realms of abstract totality, although in practice they are limited by our ability to describe them!

XXXIV

THE ULTIMATE ENTITY

We could leave it at that, with the idea of an infinite progression of abstraction, or we could say that ultimately we must arrive at an entity which is so all-embracing, of both physical and abstract realities, that it simply cannot be identified. It has absorbed all opposites, all polarities. There can be nothing outside of it, nothing which is not *it*, on any level of abstraction, and, as a result, it cannot be defined in any way.

It does not really matter whether we choose to talk of an infinite progression or of an indefinable *entity-that-is-not-an-entity*, because essentially they amount to the same "concept", which is ungraspable in its fullness by the human mind. This *entity-that-is-not-an-entity* is not "God" as commonly understood in our culture. It did not *create* the universe, it does not *control* the universe, it certainly passes no *moral judgement* on the universe and the life-forms that form part of it! It simply *embraces* the whole of the universe, the whole of everything, at all levels of abstraction, including the possibilities of existence and non-existence.

It cannot be defined by any term because it already embraces and surpasses the meaning of that term and all terms. In the same way as the tree cannot be defined in terms of the twig, this *entity-that-is-not-an-entity* cannot be defined in terms of anything on a lower level of wholeness to itself. Since *everything* is on a lower level of wholeness to itself, it cannot be defined. But, on the other hand, everything on a lower level *can* necessarily be defined in terms of this ultimate entity. The trunk of the tree *is* the tree. The physical universe *is* the *entity-that-is-not-an-entity*. A leaf on the tree *is* the tree. A mountain, a river, a deer or a frog *is* the *entity-that-is-not-an-entity*.

Human beings, too, *are* this ultimate entity. This is not just a theoretical statement – the grouping of human beings within the all-embracing set of ultimate being. It means just what it says, that we *are* the *entity-that-is-not-an-entity*. This awareness – just like the awareness that individuals *are* the collectivity or that human beings *are* nature – has been blocked by contemporary Western thinking, and blocked on many different levels.

One of the blockages surrounds the idea of "God". As already stressed, this notion as generally understood is not in any case to be confused with the idea of the *entity-that-is-not-an-entity*. A crucial difference between, for example, the standard Christian definition of "God" and this ultimate entity is that the Christian God stands outside of His creation. He does not embrace the universe so much as rule over it. While Christians do talk about their God's presence in nature and in their own hearts, there is a clear line drawn before the point at which they might say that a plant, an owl or a human being *is* God.

Our natural understanding of our belonging to the oneness of the universe has lingered on in various strands of Christian thought, over the centuries, in the form of this *pantheistic* tendency to see the divinity as immanent in the world. But this has consistently been countered by the Church as a *heretical* way of thinking. It is not hard to see why. The Church sets itself up as the means by which divine authority is enacted in the world. If that divine authority was seen as arising from within each and every human being, the Church's own role would be fatally undermined, along with the hierarchical structures of the wider social system of which it is part.

The idea of a belonging to the ultimate entity is therefore a powerful assertion of metaphysical freedom, with potentially significant social implications, *even within the erroneous conflation of this entity with the idea of divinity*. But the idea of pantheism, of God being in everything, can confuse the deeper issues at stake. While it is considered heretical by Christians, it must also be rejected by non-believers who do not accept the existence of "God" in the first place, whether or not He is seen as being immanent in all things. A term that better expresses the meaning of our being part of the ultimate entity is *panenhenism* – "*all-in-one-ism*". But at the moment the word, like the concept, is little known or understood in Western culture.

XXXV

INDIVIDUAL BEING

An even more difficult blockage to our understanding of our ultimate belonging comes from our personal understanding of who we are, as individuals.

Our entire experience of the world is subjective. We look out on the world through our personal eyes, hear through our personal ears, taste in our personal mouths and so on. We have the strong impression of dwelling solely in our own personal brains.

It is one thing to be told that we are physically part of the living Earth or that we are physically part of the stuff that makes up the universe. We can perhaps imagine how the molecules that make up our body have been recycled through the food chain, or have drifted through space before being incorporated into the organism of life on this planet. *But it is entirely another thing to be told that our deepest being does not lie within the extent of our individual presence at all.*

Can we easily accept that we are not ultimately the individual rays of life-essence streaming down into the world that we have always imagined ourselves to be, but rather parts of *one and the same shining*, divided temporarily into various beams of light by the holes in the roof of universal existence that are our individual forms?

Can we easily accept that the profoundest feeling of "I" that lies beneath all the layers of our conscious personality does not belong to us as individuals at all, but is instead something *to which we belong*, of which we are just ephemeral physical manifestations? *Is it any consolation to know that, while we never existed in quite the way we imagined, by the same token we will never die in quite the way we feared?*

The problem here is that in some ways it is very important that we see ourselves as individuals and behave as individuals. That is how living beings, particularly human beings, function. As mentioned earlier, there is a symbiotic relationship between the individual and the collectivity, on whatever scale that is. The freedom and flexibility of individual behaviour enables the collectivity to be alive in a subtle and organic way. Individuals *are* the collectivity and the collectivity simply *would not exist* without the individuals. For individuals to fulfil their potential (and thus for the collectivity to fulfil *its* potential), they *have to* be free. In order to *be* free they have to *feel* free, and in order to feel *free* they have to feel *individual*. The first phases of individual human life are about discovering and reinforcing this sense of individual existence and thus freedom.

However, we have already seen that individuals *are* in fact the collectivities which contain them, in the same way as the twig *is* in fact the tree. The impression of being *essentially* an individual is therefore *false*. We can understand why it is *necessary* to be under this illusion at a certain stage of life and for certain purposes, but it does not stop it from being an illusion.

The *being-as-individual* is merely a role being acted out, an identity being temporarily assumed by a wider entity. Ultimately, that entity is the *entity-that-is-not-an-entity* but it also manifests itself in and through all other intermediate levels of existence, such as the living organism known as Earth, the human species or various smaller collectivities.

Our sense of individual existence is a narrowing of a broader existence into the channel of our personal experience. We refract the light of this ultimate reality through the lens of our individuality and assume that we are the *source* of this light. This ungraspable ultimate reality is *defined* on the physical plane by the restraints imposed by our individual level of being – in the same way as it is defined and thus limited even at the level on which it manifests itself as the merely-physical universe. But that definition of its *shape* in no way affects its *essence*.

XXXVI

ILLUSION AND REALITY

It must be stressed here that this is a *reality* we are describing, rather than some "spiritual" fantasy. We, as individuals, can *necessarily* consist of nothing other than the stuff (physical and non-physical) of which the whole cosmos is made. There is *nothing* of us that is not part of that whole cosmos. Therefore anything that appears to be an individual essence is an illusion – *it can only in fact be the cosmic whole shaped into the appearance of an individual essence.*

This illusion of individuality – in fact of separateness from the complex living organism of which we are part – occasionally drops away and various levels of our real belonging are revealed to us. There can be a horrible loneliness involved with our existence as individuals, even when we share our day-to-day living with others. The limits of our connections to others and the limits of our own individual potential can leave us disappointed. The fragility of our own health and well-being and, above all perhaps, the inevitability of our own eventual personal death, can leave life seeming empty and absurd. Moments of connection to a supra-individual level of existence, on the other hand, tend to be associated with feelings of empowerment and joy. We can plug into that feeling in a multitude of ways, from socialising with friends to being part of a crowd with some kind of unity of purpose – a sense of *cohesion* can create a state of mind in which the individual's interests and identity are temporarily forgotten.

Many of us also stumble into a sense of belonging when we find ourselves within nature. There are *mystical* moments when we seem to stop existing as an individual and are absorbed into everything that surrounds us – trees, mountains, rivers, wildlife. This is not an *illusion* that we are experiencing, but the *falling-away* of an illusion.

At night, too, sometimes that illusion fades to nothing in the same way as the optical illusion of a blue sky that seems to limit our world. Instead, we see the reality out there – a universe of stars, planets and galaxies which are neither above us nor below us, but all around us, embracing us like the ultimate reality which we can sometimes be on the point of grasping. Music can also lift us out of the narrowness of our individual existence and up to another level of being – other forms of art, too. The *yearning* to escape the confines of our individual consciousness is real enough to prompt people to experiment with drugs or psychological techniques – whether or not these ultimately work is not the point.

In the end the only sure way of finding that connection with supra-individual existence is to consolidate our fleeting *mystical* experiences of wider belonging with a more permanent *gnosis* – the knowledge that this existence is real and primary. In order to function as human beings, we cannot completely abandon the awareness of our existence on an individual level – that would be like trying to drive a car without sitting in the driver's seat. But what we can achieve is a *near-simultaneous awareness of both individual and supra-individual levels of existence*, the same oscillation that we encountered in considering the social relationship between individual and collectivity.

XXXVII

FALSE TRAILS

It was mentioned earlier that the initial phases of human life are concerned with creating the necessary independence of human individuality. The process of surpassing that individual level follows on from that both in terms of sequence – it comes *after* the creation of independence – and in terms of causality – it is *made possible by* the creation of individual independence.

It would be a mistake for an individual to try to lose their sense of individuality before they had fully gained it in the first place, although this might superficially seem like a useful short-cut. It is the oscillation between individual presence and collective presence that is the key to the natural functioning and freedom of human beings and a full oscillation would not be possible if it were impeded on one side by an incomplete sense of being.

In a natural – pre-state, pre-industrial – human society, the transition between the nurturing of individuality and the assumption of wider collective responsibility might manifest as a *rite of passage* from one phase of personal development to the next.

In contemporary society, this transition is blocked or distorted. Because individuality is regarded as the sole basis for existence, there can be no progression to a stage in which this is merged symbiotically with the interests of the collectivity. Instead, on a social level, individual self-interest is retained as the primary motivating factor and set against the demands of the fake collectivities of authority. On a metaphysical level, our sense of separate individual existence is never transcended, with damaging effects on the mental well-being of the individual and, thus, on the broader collective entities.

As we have seen, this does not mean that people do not yearn for that wider sense of belonging and that they do not often seek it out in various ways. Sometimes they specifically seek out a "spiritual" path to take them beyond a purely individual sense of existence. However, there are potentially still numerous blockages and distortions in the way. Sometimes, for instance, spiritual paths are presented merely as tools for personal self-strengthening and self-advancement outside of any social context, thus merely reinforcing an individualist approach to life. On other occasions, they might propose surrender of individuality not to any organic level of collective existence, but to an artificial collectivity invented by those peddling this "spiritual" approach – the hierarchical structures of organised religions or cults.

XXXVIII

UNDERSTANDING OBSCURED

It is not by chance that our culture lays down so many false trails to be followed by those seeking to know and embrace the reality of their own supra-individual existence: the suppression of that knowledge is essential to the continuation of that culture, that system.

People who understand that they are not merely individuals, but also *are* the collectivities to which they belong, are not going to allow this living freedom to be denied by the dead hand of "property", "law" or "nation". People who understand that their individual freedom is also the freedom of the collectivity will not feel any need to conform to that collectivity's existing point of view, since they know that *their dissent is entirely part of the organic collective decision-*

making process.

People who understand that they are not just *surrounded* by nature but that they *are* nature, will not sit back and watch that nature destroyed in the name of humanity's allegedly separate self-interest. People who understand that they *are* the ultimate reality of the universe will not imagine that their own individual mortality makes their existence meaningless or *absurd*. They are neither going to be fooled by phoney gods demanding cowed obedience, nor so gripped by the fear of *individual death* that they shirk the full collective responsibilities of *individual life.*

All this understanding challenges, on many levels, the assumptions of our current society and therefore cannot co-exist with them. Ideas and attitudes are thus spawned by the system/process to obscure this understanding, often by the false conflation of fundamentally different concepts.

The notion of collective identity is conflated with the notion of nation or state, and thus presented as the *opposite of* individual freedom. Nature is conflated with the idea of a false "natural order" as used to describe the shape of hierarchical societies of the recent past and accordingly the idea of "nature" is itself treated as inherently reactionary. Similarly, the idea of innate human qualities – the qualities that enable us to live free of external control – is conflated with the idea of externally-defined restrictions on individual human potential, such as in the suggestion that certain people are "innately" suited to a certain social role. In reaction to this, everything to do with humanity – character, potential, culture – is regarded instead as an artificial construct and thus the notion of humanity being an organic entity becomes unthinkable.

The original ideas and meanings behind words are lost when they are used to describe other phenomena. How can we describe and promote real "democracy" if that word is generally understood to refer to the system of political representation that already exists? How can we demand "freedom" when it has been redefined to describe that which we already have?

The process goes much deeper into our dominant culture. The separation of words from their origin and significance is increasingly taken to the point where we can barely imagine that there lies anything behind them at all. This is not just the policing of our thoughts, but the *preventative policing* of possible thoughts! The idea of a *universal essence* cannot even be recognised, let alone discussed, as both its component factors are ascribed zero validity. The idea of mind is replaced by that of behaviour and any trace of the psyche surgically removed from psychology. The very concept of philosophy is detached from the metaphysical search for truth and shunted into the dead-end sidings of self-referential semantics. Even the concept of "meaning" is seen as having no meaning. Any way of thinking outside this ever-narrowing framework becomes impossible in a *post-natural, post-human, post-authentic* intellectual climate that effectively constitutes a complete *paralysis* of the collective human mind.

IXL

UNITY OF MEANING

As we have noted before in a different context, it is important that we understand that these blockages exist and that we understand *why* these blockages exist – that they are the intellectual phenomena by which the dominant system/process hides the reality of its existence and simultaneously stifles understanding of the means by which it does so.

It is *impossible* to understand this without also understanding what the system/process is and how it came into existence in the first place. If we do not understand what the system/process is and what it is doing, we will not understand the *deliberate* nature of the mental obstacles placed in our way – again, we must emphasise that we mean deliberate on the part of the *system/process* rather on the part of any particular individuals.

If we do not understand what the system/process is, we will not be able properly to address and challenge the extent of its power. At the best we might be able to individually bypass some of its blockages, but it will remain firmly intact.

Suppose, for instance, an interest in metaphysics led a man to discover the insight that we are all essentially part of the ultimate all-embracing cosmos. In itself, this is a key discovery and this gnosis ought to open the way to understanding of the human condition on all levels. It should expand itself "downwards" to bring this man a knowledge of our belonging to nature and to genuine collectivities, and with that an understanding of the falsity of fake collectivities like the nation and state, and the falsity of the idea of a purely individual social existence.

But we would be reckoning here without the existence of the obstacles, the blockages, thrown up in the man's path by the system/process. For a start, the blocked thinking which it encourages involves a rigid compartmentalisation of areas of reflection. Any conclusions he reached under the heading "metaphysics" would not be allowed to leach through into the areas headed "environmental studies" or "sociology".

It is not so much that all of us are *bound* by

these labels and limitations, but that the dominant discourse in our society – that which takes place in the universities and in the pages of various journals and media – is defined by them and any approaches that do not coincide with these assumptions are marginalised to the extent that they have little chance of affecting society.

If the man wanted to fully explain his understanding of the human condition, he would therefore at the same time have to break free from these specific blockages. To justify this, he would also have to challenge their existence and to outline the limitations they would otherwise have imposed on his work. He might also want to explore their probable causes and examine other related blockages which, according to his analysis, had prevented a wider understanding of the human condition as he described it. These thought-blockages would necessarily go beyond the immediate ones concerning the theme of his work and take in *the blockages which had allowed a society to evolve and thrive in which it had become pragmatically necessary to block certain social and metaphysical understandings.*

If this man decides *not* to do that, if he opts for the easier path of confining his analysis to the realm of metaphysics, he may succeed in securing interest in his work from within that field, but he will have failed on a larger scale. He

will have failed to communicate the full
ramifications of what he describes and thus also
failed to communicate the areas in which
thought-blockages need to be removed in order
for what he describes to be fully comprehended.
He will have achieved nothing in broader terms.
Furthermore, by accepting that his work must be
limited to a narrow field and cut off from
everything else, he is tacitly accepting the
dominant perception that there is no overall
unity of meaning to existence.

If he argues that it is possible to consider
human beings as part of the cosmos but *not* to
also consider them as part of the planet, the
human species or other localised collectivities,
then he is betraying the very insight from which
he started. *He has himself become part of the
blockage.* He has added another layer on to the
multitude of layers that already conceal from us
our true nature. He has allowed himself to act as
part of the system/process and has effectively
disabled his own individual freedom to act
against the continuation of that system.

An understanding of the *metaphysical*
reality of human existence is therefore
meaningless without a grasping of the *political*
reality. Approaches to metaphysics or
"spirituality" which refuse to consider the
political reality – in the broadest sense of its
meaning – are empty and cut off from their own

significance. They can end up, for instance, suggesting that an individual can achieve personal enlightenment outside of any social context, or even proposing that in order to achieve personal enlightenment on a metaphysical level an individual has to turn their back on intermediate levels of collective belonging. By ignoring the whole issue of the blockages and the system/process that has erected them in order to enable its own continuation, these approaches ultimately suggest that we *do not have to challenge that system*, that we can achieve metaphysical, and thus general, freedom *within the structures of that system*.

This is a very comfortable position to hold, as it involves little danger of confrontation with authority. The system is well able to incorporate a quarantined approach to metaphysical freedom which has no impact at all on the functioning of its various layers of exploitation and deceit. Indeed, the abandonment of the social context in favour of a *purely metaphysical* level of consciousness can only strengthen the power of that dominant system.

XL

LIMITED THINKING

Suppose now that that same man has *not* directed his research towards a metaphysical level of knowledge – perhaps because he has seen that it is generally contemplated outside of any political and social context.

Instead, he focuses his enquiries on the material conditions in which humans find themselves in contemporary society. He comes to an understanding of the way human beings, deprived of the physical and cultural base of land-belonging, have been forced into material and psychological dependence on the system which exploits them. He understands that individuals depend on communal co-operation for their survival and he would almost claim that mutual aid forms part of innate human nature.

However, he has learnt that there is no such thing as human nature, or anything innate at all, because human behaviour and culture are entirely determined by the external environment. Rather than expose himself to hostility and ridicule by contradicting this received wisdom, he turns his back on any such thread of thought and concentrates his analysis on a purely social level.

While he certainly regards the human species as an important concept, it does not occur to him that it might be a physical living organism. Nature, for him, is the environment – something that surrounds humanity rather than something of which humanity is part. And the idea of a cosmic *entity-which-is-not-an-entity* registers with him only as a disguised form of ridiculous religious superstition distracting people from social realities. Since these various types of organic collective existence cannot even be considered by him, from within the limits of his narrowed thinking, it follows that any connection between them is not merely invisible to him, but impossible for him to even to *begin* to conceive of.

By blocking his own possible understanding of a wider reality, and confining his analysis to one level only, he confirms and reinforces the thought-separation that pushed him in that direction. *He has himself become part of the blockage*. He has added another layer on to the multitude of layers that already conceal from us our true nature. He has allowed himself to act as part of the system/process and has effectively disabled his own individual freedom to act against the continuation of that system.

From whatever angle the man approaches a possible understanding of the overall reality, the inherent thought-restrictions of the dominant system will potentially block his success. We can see that these blockages are complex and multi-layered and thus difficult to grasp – and *that this difficulty itself creates another layer of blockage!* This is not a question here of a simple fascist-style state in which it is forbidden to express certain ideas. In our culture, it becomes *impossible* to express certain ideas because they make no sense within a context which has arisen precisely in order to prevent them being expressed.

XLI

DISPELLING DELUSION

A collective delusion has taken over humanity, fogged its mind, rendered it incapable of understanding its own essential reality or the way in which it has become blinded to that reality and thus incapable of acting in its own real interests.

Overcoming delusion forms part of the "spiritual" path which individuals can take in order to discover their ultimate reality. To dispel delusion, all the layers of that delusion have to be stripped away, all the assumptions built up around the ego as being the true and only source of individual being. Only when the vessel of the human mind has been emptied of the stagnant water of falsehood is it then able to be filled instead from the fresh fountains of truth.

Overcoming delusion must necessarily also be the collective aim of humankind if it is to rediscover its connection to reality – its sanity, in fact. This will not simply involve dismantling the physical infrastructure of domination but also every layer of the supporting delusion, with all its assumptions, blockages, denials and deceits.

What will come first? Individuals who have rid themselves of delusion and therefore can encourage humanity as a whole to do the same? Or will it only be after the collective delusion has been dispelled that individuals will also be freed? Neither can come first, as both must happen simultaneously. After all, collectivities *are* individuals and individuals *are* collectivities.

This is no small task to contemplate! We have already seen how deeply delusion is embedded in the minds of individuals and of society. It can be seen on every level of existence from the denial of metaphysical unity to the acceptance of the deceit of land "ownership", from the denial of the idea of innate human nature to the acceptance of fake collectivities replacing the organic reality. Ridding ourselves of all of this amounts to a lot more than mere reform.

On the individual level, the process of stripping away the ego is often regarded as a kind of metaphorical suicide. It is not a *real* suicide, of course, because its aim is not death but the creation of fresh, renewed life. In the same way, our culture, our civilization, needs to undergo a metaphorical suicide. This will not be a *real* suicide, of course, because its aim is not the death of humanity but its renewal, its regeneration. *Its aim is the restoration of our natural freedom.*

XLII

ABSTRACT REALITY

From the perspective of the dominant way of thinking, the point which we have now theoretically reached appears to be a complete dead end. Clearing away all the structures of thought and culture from which our contemporary reality has been constructed seems like a recklessly dangerous course of action. It amounts to nothing but a "descent into anarchy" and can only result in humanity "reverting to barbarism" with all the horrors that this implies.

But this is only how the situation looks from within the delusion itself. *Any call to do away with certain assumptions is always going to look insane from a point of view still based on those very assumptions!*

The assumption that there is no innate

146

nature to things at all leads to the conclusion that the removal of the existing system and all its delusions would leave a vacuum which would not *naturally* be filled by anything at all, other than perhaps the chaos which this thinking invariably associates with the lack of artificial structure. To rid ourselves of this assumption – as we must do if we are to embark on a course of action which it regards as absurd – is to accept that this vacuum *would* be naturally filled by something and that there *is* an innate nature to things.

This concept of an innate nature goes beyond the question of collective solidarity and even that of human belonging to the living planetary organism. In fact, we can trace its origins to the higher levels of metaphysical abstraction which were addressed earlier. We saw that the reality of something's physical existence is necessarily contained within the idea of the possibility of its physical existence. This possibility is in turn contained within the idea of the potential for the possibility of its existence (and, therefore, the potential for the impossibility of its existence).

We saw that the concept of three-ness, for instance, does not depend on the physical existence of three actual physical things. It allows us to consider three of anything, to various degrees of abstraction. Three sounds, for instance, or three smells, three dreams, three ideas, three dimensions, three thirteens. The same is true of any concept. We can grasp the concept of a ten-foot long purple flying banana, without it actually existing, or indeed it even having the *possibility* of actually existing. The very fact that we have imagined it gives it some kind of existence, even though in this case this is on a plane more abstract than even the possibility of existence – it perhaps "exists" or *subsists* on the level of the potential possibility or impossibility of its existence. While our ability to imagine its possible existence is undoubtedly drawn from our experience of actual physical objects, the abstract existence of this particular concept, like the concept of three-ness, is *not dependent on its own existence on a physical plane.*

All possible physical realities (and impossible ones) must necessarily already exist on an abstract level. The possibility of something existing is a prerequisite for its existence. This is not a question of sequence in terms of time (which is not relevant here) but of the relationship of dependence between one and the other. Existence depends on the possibility of existence, whereas the possibility of existence does not depend on actual physical existence.

Given that these abstract concepts exist without the need for a corresponding physical reality, any vacuum created by the removal of an existing system (physical or mental) would not in fact be a vacuum on an abstract level. It would still retain the invisible structure of possibilities that permeates the universe at every level. The removal of one particular reality (the current system) would then make possible the *coming-into-physical-existence* of another reality which until then had only "existed" in abstraction.

XLIII

FORMS WITHOUT CONTENT

But what does this mean? Does it imply that *any* abstract concept may now be converted into physical reality, including such absurd notions as flying purple bananas and chaotic social collapse resulting from the absence of authority? No, it doesn't – because if possibilities are to exist on the plane of physical existence they must conform to the limitations imposed by that plane. We could say that there are certain *rules* involved in manifestation on any particular plane of being. These are not externally-imposed rules but *inherent rules*, related to a certain way of being which a concept must necessarily assume if it is to be able to show itself, to become real, in that context.

It will have to reduce itself in some way to

allow itself to exist on that level of existence. A three-dimensional object, like a sphere, can be *represented* on a purely two-dimensional plane but cannot exist there in its fullness. It does not matter whether it is simply rendered as a simple circle, or whether by use of optical illusion it is given an apparently three-dimensional shape – it must still exist within the limits of two-dimensionality.

Concepts of potentiality and possibility cannot transfer themselves to the plane of physical existence unless they conform to the *rules* of that particular physical reality (there may be other realities of which we are unaware). These rules, as they have been called here thus far, are themselves among the "things" which exist on a potential level and which then manifest in physical existence. They do not manifest in terms of solid physicality, like an apple or a chair, but they nevertheless manifest – as part of the very *structure* of the physical world. We could also choose to call these rules *forms* – if we understand that they are the form itself, the guiding principle, rather than the *content* of the form, the physical matter that takes up that shape according to their guidance.

These forms are an essential constituent of the plane of physical existence and are the means by which possibilities *become* reality. The universe, including the abstract levels beyond physical reality, is one single entity and as such possesses a structure of its own. The forms are part of that structure, that pattern, that inherent fabric that holds the universe together and that underlies all levels and all connections between levels.

On our level of existence, we can detect the presence of these forms in various ways. They are, for example, the principle of a physical object's *extension* – the physical space it takes up in our world. They also are the principle of *quantity* – and, within that, of two-ness, three-ness, thirteen-ness and so on. They are also the principle of shape. Consider snowflakes, for instance. Each one is entirely unique and yet the shape of each is determined by the same guiding rules. Again, it is not the *content* that is determined, but the way that content is *structured*.

Mountains can only exist in our physical reality if their forms conform to the rules of our reality, such as gravity – they cannot float in mid-air, even though the concept of such a mountain can subsist on an abstract level. The forms are a kind of filter through which possibilities must inevitably pass before they can come to exist on the physical plane, bearing in mind the rules by which that physical plane operates. Rivers can only run downhill. Wood floats. Bananas do not fly.

These innate forms apply to everything. It is part of the inherent nature of ivy, for instance, that it will try to grow along a wall. It may not actually do so – there may be no wall for it to grow along, or it may be chopped back before it has the chance – but the tendency remains in its nature. Human beings have an innate capacity to be able to hold and manipulate objects. That doesn't mean that we can do so as soon as we are born, or that some human beings are *not* able to use their hands in this way, but it remains part of our human nature that we have the theoretical *capacity* to do so, even if that is thwarted by circumstance. The same applies to the ability to use language. We have the innate capacity to do so. This does not mean we have the knowledge of a particular language in our minds when we are born, or that we will *necessarily* ever learn to use a language. There is no actual *content* to this form. It is merely a capacity, a structure that makes it *possible* for our use of language to become a reality.

These innate qualities cannot logically be challenged. We *must* have the inherent *capacity* to be able to manipulate objects, and to learn language, or else *we would not be able to do so*. We *must* have the inherent *capacity* to be able to filter information, analyse reality, construct arguments – otherwise we would *not be able to do so*.

XLIV

THE FREEDOM TO BE ALIVE

It is in this context that we must consider the innate capacity of human beings to live together co-operatively and without hierarchical structures being imposed on them. This capacity is as real as the capacity to use our hands and to talk to each other. It is part of the very essence of the human species. The species is a living organism and thus has an innate ability to *function*. Its component parts have evolved to work in subtle harmony with each other in order to ensure its survival. There can no more exist a human species *without* the capacity for co-operation than there can exist a mountain which can float in mid-air, or a triangular snowflake. That is what the human species *is*.

The existence of this *capacity* obviously does

not mean that we *must necessarily* live that way
– we only need to look around us today for proof
of that. But it does mean that we are *able* to live
that way and, moreover, that, in the absence of
any factors preventing us from doing so, we *will*
live that way. Human life will operate according
to its own innate structures, unless it is
prevented from doing so. With the removal of our
unfree system – consisting of all the various
factors that prevent us living freely – human
society will naturally be co-operative. There will
be no vacuum, there will be no chaos – there will
just be the crystallisation of human nature
according to the invisible structures innate to its
reality.

Freedom is involved in this process in two
distinct ways. Firstly, it will be freedom in its
dynamic aspect – *the innate human desire for
freedom* – that will act as the battering ram to
destroy the current system. Freedom here takes
the form of energy, life-force, creating the
possibility of transformation. Secondly, when the
various blockages and delusions which imprison
us have been cleared away, freedom in its
permanent fullness will then be able to flourish.

By removing all the impediments to our
natural modes of behaviour we will thus finally
have reached the point where the limited,
negatively-formed concept of *freedom-from* has
been surpassed and we are connected directly to

the positive *freedom-to* that lies behind it.

What is that *freedom-to*? Simply the freedom to exist as we are meant to, as our nature allows us to, as the inherent form of humanity tells us to. The freedom, as individuals, to be individual – to fulfil our responsibility of being unique, unpredictable, uncontrollable, and thus maintain the species as a living, evolving, self-adjusting organism. The freedom as collectivities to function properly, to embrace the symbiotic relationship with individuality, to be steered by the subtle inner workings of our authentic democracy. The freedom as a species to be aware of all this, to understand our essence, to understand that we *have* an essence and that it permeates every level of our existence. The freedom as a planet to breathe, to remain healthy, to have the full unsuppressed use of our organic immune system to fight off any diseases that threaten to wipe us out. All of this arises from, and feeds into, our freedom as the ultimate *entity-that-is-not-an-entity* to embrace the paradox of being both infinite, timeless, ungraspable and also – through physical manifestation – limited, mortal, solid. In short, on all levels, *the freedom to be alive.*

Is that really too much to ask for?

BACKGROUND BIBLIOGRAPHY

Against Civilization: Readings and Reflections, ed. by John Zerzan, (Eugene, Oregon: Uncivilized Books, 1999)

The Anarchist Reader, ed. by George Woodcock, (Glasgow: Fontana, 1986)

Michael Bakunin, *The Political Philosophy of Bakunin: Scientific Anarchism*, ed. by G.P. Maximoff, (New York: The Free Press of Glencoe, 1964)

Anne Bancroft, *Modern Mystics and Sages,* (London & St Albans: Paladin, 1978)

Jean Baudrillard, *La société de consommation, ses mythes, ses structures*, (Paris: Folio, 2011)

Sharon Beder, *Global Spin: The Corporate Assault on Environmentalism,* (Totnes: Green Books, 2002)

Walter Benjamin, *Illuminations*, ed. by Hannah Arendt, trans. by Harry Zohn, (London: Jonathan Cape, 1970)

Ernst Bloch, *Thomas Münzer, théologien de la révolution*, trans. by Maurice de Gandillac, (Paris: Les Prairies ordinaires, 2012)

David Bohm, *Wholeness and the Implicate Order*, (Abingdon: Routledge, 2002)

Dee Brown, *Bury My Heart at Wounded Knee: An Indian History of the American West,* (London: Vintage, 1991)

Gerald Bullett, *The English Mystics,* (London: Michael Joseph, 1950)

Joseph Campbell, *The Hero With a Thousand Faces*, (London: Fontana Press, 1993)

Joseph Campbell, *The Masks of God* series, (London: Souvenir Press, 2011)

Fritjof Capra, *The Tao of Physics: An exploration of the parallels between modern physics and Eastern mysticism,* (London: Flamingo, 1992)

Noam Chomsky, *Chomsky on Anarchism*, ed. by Barry Pateman, (Edinburgh, Oakland & West Virginia, AK Press, 2005)

Voltairine de Cleyre, *The Voltairine de Cleyre Reader*, ed. by A.J. Brigati, (Oakland & Edinburgh: AK Press, 2004)

Ananada K. Coomaraswamy, *The Transformation of Nature in Art,* (New York: Dover, 1956)

Paul Cudenec, *The Anarchist Revelation: Being What We're Meant To Be,* (Sussex: Winter Oak, 2013)

Paul Cudenec, *Antibodies, Anarchangels and Other Essays,* (Sussex: Winter Oak, 2013)

Paul Cudenec, *The Stifled Soul of Humankind,* (Sussex: Winter Oak, 2014)

Yves Delhoysie & Georges Lapierre, *L'Incendie millénariste,* (Paris: Os Cangaceiros, 2011)

Divertir pour dominer: La culture de masse contre les peuples, (Montreuil: Editions L'Echappée, 2010)

Mircea Eliade, *Myths, Dreams and Mysteries: The*

Encounter Between Contemporary Faiths and Archaic Reality, trans. by Philip Mairet, (London: Collins, 1974)

Existentialism from Dostoevsky to Sartre, ed. by Walter Kaufmann, (New York: Meridian, 1972)

Johannes Fabricius, *Alchemy: The Medieval Alchemists and their Royal Art*, (London: Diamond Books, 1994)

Majid Fakhry, *Islamic Philosophy: A Beginner's Guide*, (Oxford: Oneworld Publications, 2009)

Fascism: A Reader's Guide, ed. by Walter Laqueur, (Aldershot, Scolar Press, 1991)

Emma Goldman, *Living My Life*, (London: Duckworth, 1932)

René Guénon, *The Crisis of the Modern World*, trans. by Arthur Osborne, Marco Pallis & Richard C. Nicholson, (Ghent NY: Sophia Perennis, 2001)

René Guénon, *East and West*, trans. by Martin Lings, (Hillsdale NY: Sophia Perennis, 2001)

René Guénon, *Introduction to the Study of the Hindu Doctrines*, trans. by Marco Pallis, (Hillsdale, NY: Sophia Perennis, 2004)

René Guénon, *Man and His Becoming According to the Vedānta*, trans. by Richard C. Nicholson, (Hillsdale, NY: Sophia Perennis, 2004)

René Guénon, *The Multiple States of the Being*, trans. by Henry D. Fohr, (Hillsdale, NY: Sophia Perennis, 2004)

René Guénon, *The Reign of Quantity and the Signs of the Times*, translated by Lord Northbourne, (Hillsdale NY: Sophia Perennis, 2004)

Andrew Harvey, *The Way of Passion: A Celebration of Rumi*, (New York: Jeremy P. Tarcher/Putnam, 2001)

Dr Ali Hassan Abdel-Kader, *The Life, Personality and Writings of Al-Junayd: A Study of a Third/Ninth Century Mystic*, (London: Luzac, 1976)

Hermetica: The Ancient Greek and Latin Writings Which Contain Religious or Philosophical Teachings Ascribed to Hermes Trismegistus, ed. and trans. by Walter Scott, (Shaftesbury: Solos Press, 1997)

Hermann Hesse, *The Glass Bead Game*, (London: Vintage Books, 2000)

Herman Hesse, *Siddharta*, (London: Picador, 1973)

Christopher Hill, *The World Turned Upside Down: Radical Ideas During the English Revolution*, (London: Pelican, 1975)

James Hillman: *Archetypal Psychology: A Brief Account*, (Dallas: Spring Publications, 1990)

Stephan A. Hoeller, *The Gnostic Jung and the Seven Sermons to the Dead*, (Wheaton IL: Quest, 1994)

Aldous Huxley, *Brave New World Revisited*, (London: Chatto and Windus, 1959)

Aldous Huxley, *The Perennial Philosophy*, (London: Chatto & Windus, 1980)

I Am Not A Man, I Am Dynamite: Friedrich Nietzsche and the Anarchist Tradition, ed. by John Moore with Spencer Sunshine, (Brooklyn, New York: Autonomedia, 2004)

Ibn Al-Husayn Al-Sulami, *The Book of Sufi Chivalry: Lessons to a Son of the Moment, Futuwwah*, (London, East West Publications, 1983)

Ibn 'Arabi, *Journey to the Lord of Power*, (London and The Hague: East West Publications, 1981)

The Invisible Committee (Comité invisible), *A nos amis*, (Paris: La Fabrique, 2014)

The Invisible Committee, *The Coming Insurrection*,

(http://tarnac9.wordpress.com/texts/the-coming-insurrection, 2007)

Karl Jaspers, *Man in the Modern Age,* trans. by Eden and Cedar Paul, (London: Routledge & Kegan Paul, 1951)

Karl Jaspers, *The Perennial Scope of Philosophy,* trans. by Ralph Manheim, (London: Routledge & Kegan Paul, 1950)

Richard Jefferies, *The Story of My Heart: My Autobiography,* (Sussex: Winter Oak Press, 2015)

Derrick Jensen, *Dreams,* (New York: Seven Stories Press, 2011)

Derrick Jensen, *Endgame, Vols I & II,* (New York: Seven Stories Press, 2006)

Derrick Jensen and Aric McBay, *What We Leave Behind,* (New York: Seven Stories Press, 2009)

C. G. Jung, *Modern Man in Search of a Soul,* (London and Henley: Routledge & Kegan Paul, 1978)

C.G. Jung, *Psyche & Symbol: A Selection from the Writings of C.G. Jung,* ed. by Violet S. de Laszlo, (New York: Anchor Books, 1958)

C.G. Jung, *Psychology and Alchemy,* (London: Routledge, 1989)

C.G. Jung, *Symbols of Transformation,* (New Jersey: Princeton University Press, 1967)

Franz Kafka, *The Trial and Metamorphosis,* (London: Landmark, 1983)

Anton Kielce, *Le soufisme,* (Paris: M.A. Editions, 1984)

Peter Kropotkin, *Kropotkin's Revolutionary Pamphlets: A Collection of Writings by Peter Kropotkin,* ed. by Roger N. Baldwin, (New York: Dover Publications, 1970)

Peter Kropotkin, *Mutual Aid: A Factor of Evolution*, (London: Freedom Press, 1993)

Gustav Landauer, *For Socialism*, trans. by David J. Parent, (St Louis: Telos Press, 1978)

Gustav Landauer, *Revolution and Other Writings: A Political Reader*, ed. and trans. by Gabriel Kuhn, (Oakland: PM Press, 2010)

Lao Tzu, *Tao Te Ching*, (Harmondsworth: Penguin, 1963)

Bernard Lazare, *La Question Juive,* (Paris: Editions Allia, 2012)

Martin Lings, *What is Sufism?,* (London: George Allen & Unwin Ltd, 1975)

David Lorimer, *Whole in One: The Near-Death Experience and the Ethic of Interconnectedness*, (London: Arkana, 1990)

Michael Löwy, *Juifs hétérdoxes: Romantisme, messianisme, utopie,* (Paris: Éditions de l' éclat; 2010)

Michael Löwy, *Rédemption et utopie: le judaïsme libertaire en Europe centrale,* (Paris: Éditions du Sandre, 2009)

Managing Democracy, Managing Dissent: Capitalism, Democracy and the Organisation of Consent, ed. by Rebecca Fisher, (London: Corporate Watch, 2013)

Eugène Marais, *The Soul of the Ape,* (London: Anthony Blond Ltd, 1969)

Eugène Marais, *The Soul of the White Ant,* (London: Jonathan Cape, 1971)

Herbert Marcuse, *One Dimensional Man: Studies in the Ideology of Advanced Industrial Society*, (London: Routledge & Kegan Paul, 1964)

Henry Margenau, *The Miracle of Existence*, (Boston and London: Shambhala, 1987)

Peter Marshall, *Demanding the Impossible: A History of Anarchism,* (London: Fontana Press, 1993)

Peter Marshall, *The Philosopher's Stone: A Quest for the Secrets of Alchemy,* (London: Pan Books, 2002)

Peter Marshall, *Riding the Wind: A New Philosophy for a New Era,* (London: Continuum, 2000)

Peter Marshall, *William Blake: Visionary Anarchist,* (London: Freedom Press, 2008)

Charles B. Maurer, *Call to Revolution. The Mystical Anarchism of Gustav Landauer,* (Detroit: Wayne State University Press, 1971)

Frank McLynn, *Carl Gustav Jung,* (New York: St Martin's Griffin, 1998)

Meister Eckhart, ed. by Halcyon Backhouse, (London: Hodder & Stoughton, 1992)

William Morris, *News From Nowhere and Selected Writings and Designs,* ed. by Asa Briggs, (London: Penguin, 1984)

Reynold A. Nicholson, *The Mystics of Islam,* (London: Routledge & Kegan Paul, 1979)

Friedrich Nietzsche, *Thus Spoke Zarathustra: A Book for Everyone and No One,* trans. by R.J. Hollingdale, (London: Penguin, 1977)

Friedrich Nietzsche, *Twilight of the Idols and The Anti-Christ,* trans. by R.J. Hollingdale, (London: Penguin, 1968)

Kit Pedler, *The Quest for Gaia: A Book of Changes,* (London: Granada, 1981)

Fredy Perlman, *Against His-story, Against Leviathan!* (Detroit, Black and Red, 1983)

John Prebble, *The Highland Clearances,* (London: Penguin, 1976)

Herbert Read, *The Forms of Things Unknown: Essays*

Towards An Aesthetic Philosophy, (New York: Horizon Press, 1960)

Eliseé Reclus, *Histoire d'un ruisseau,* (Arles: Actes Sud, 1995)

Religious Anarchism: New Perspectives, ed. by Alexandre J.M.E. Christoyannapoulos, (Newcastle: Cambridge Scholars Publishing, 2009)

Robin Robertson, *Jungian Archetypes: Jung, Gödel, and the History of Archetypes,* (York Beach, Maine: Nicolas-Hays, 1995)

Rudolf Rocker, *Anarcho-Syndicalism,* (London: Pluto Press, 1989)

John Ruskin, *The Genius of John Ruskin: Selections from his Writings,* ed. by John D. Rosenberg, (London: George Allen & Unwin Ltd, 1964)

Marshall Sahlins, *Stone Age Economics,* (London: Routledge, 2004)

Kirkpatrick Sale, *After Eden: The Evolution of Human Domination,* (Durham and London: Duke University Press, 2006)

Kirkpatrick Sale, *Rebels Against the Future,* (London: Quartet Books, 1996)

Kirkpatrick Sale, *The Conquest of Paradise: Christopher Columbus and the Columbian Legacy,* (London: Papermac, 1992)

Linda Schierse Leonard, *Witness to the Fire: Creativity and the Veil of Addiction,* (Boston and London: Shambhala, 1990)

Frithjof Schuon, *The Transcendent Unity of Religions,* trans. by Peter Townsend, (London: Faber & Faber, 1953)

Idries Shah, *The Sufis,* (London: W.H. Allen & Co, 1977)

Rupert Sheldrake, *The Sense of Being Stared At*, (London: Arrow Books, 2004)

Rupert Sheldrake, *The Rebirth of Nature: The Greening of Science and God*, (London: Rider, 1991)

Paul Shepard, *Nature and Madness*, (Athens, USA: University of Georgia Press, 1998)

Herbert Silberer, *Hidden Symbolism of Alchemy and the Occult Arts*, trans. by Smith Ely Jelliffe, (New York: Dover, 1971)

June Singer, *Boundaries of the Soul: The Practice of Jung's Psychology*, (New York: Anchor Books, 1989)

June Singer, *The Unholy Bible: Blake, Jung and the Collective Unconscious*, (Boston, USA: Sigo Press, 1986)

Margaret Smith, *The Way of the Mystics: The Early Christian Mystics and the Rise of the Sufis*, (London: Sheldon Press, 1976)

Oswald Spengler, *The Decline of the West*, (Oxford: Oxford University Press, 1991)

Murray Stein, *In Midlife: A Jungian Perspective*, (Dallas: Spring Publications, 1983)

E.P. Thompson, *Customs in Common*, (London: Penguin, 1993)

E.P. Thompson, *The Making of the English Working Class*, (Harmondsworth: Penguin, 1978)

Henry Thoreau, *The Portable Thoreau*, ed. by Carl Bode, (London: Penguin, 1979)

Paul Tillich, *The Courage to Be*, (London and Glasgow: Fontana, 1973)

Eckhart Tolle, *A New Earth. Awakening to your life's purpose*, (London: Penguin, 2006)

Leo Tolstoy, *A Calendar of Wisdom*, (London: Hodder & Stoughton, 1998)

Leo Tolstoy, *Life*, (London: Walter Scott, n.d.)

Raoul Vaneigem, *Les Hérésies,* (Paris: *Que sais-je?*, Presses Universitaires de France)

David Watson, *Against The Megamachine: Essays on Empire and Its Enemies,* (Brooklyn, NY: Autonomedia, 1998)

Alan Watts, *The Book On the Taboo Against Knowing Who You Are,* (London: Souvenir, 2012)

Alan Watts, *Tao: The Watercourse Way*, with the collaboration of Al Chung-Liang Huang, (London, Arkana, 1992)

Alan Watts, *The Wisdom of Insecurity,* (London: Rider & Co, 1978)

Colin Wilson, *The Outsider*, (London: Victor Gollancz, 1956)

Colin Wilson, *Religion and the Rebel*, (London: Victor Gollancz, 1957)

George Woodcock, *Anarchism*, (London: Penguin, 1979)

George Woodcock, *Herbert Read: The Stream and the Source,* (Montreal/New York/London: Black Rose Books, 2008)

Marion Woodman and Elinor Dickson, *Dancing In the Flames: The Dark Goddess in the Transformation of Consciousness*, (Boston: Shambhala, 1997)

John Zerzan, *Elements of Refusal,* (Columbia, MO: C.A.L. Press, 1999)

John Zerzan, *Future Primitive and Other Essays*, (Camberley: Green Anarchist Books, 1996)

John Zerzan, *Running on Emptiness: The Pathology of Civilization*, (Los Angeles: Feral House, 2002)

John Zerzan, *Twilight of the Machines,* (Port Townsend WA: Feral House, 2008)

Also from Winter Oak

THE STIFLED SOUL OF HUMANKIND

PAUL CUDENEC

Paul Cudenec depicts a humanity dispossessed, a society in which freedom, autonomy, creativity, culture, and the spirit of collective solidarity have been deliberately suffocated by a ruthlessly violent and exploitative elite. But he also identifies an underground current of heresy and resistance which resurfaces at key moments in history and which, he argues, has the primal strength to carry us forward to a future of vitality and renewal.

"We have to reintroduce ourselves to history, not as observers but as participants. The power that we can rediscover in ourselves is, among other things, the power to create the future. Prophecy brings hope, hope brings courage, courage brings action, action brings inspiration, inspiration brings more determination, renewed hope, deepened courage. Once this magical spiral of revolt has started spinning, it takes on a life of its own."

Also from Winter Oak

THE ANARCHIST REVELATION

PAUL CUDENEC

Paul Cudenec draws on an impressively wide range of authors to depict a corrupted civilization on the brink of self-destruction and to call for a powerful new philosophy of resistance and renewal. He combines the anarchism of the likes of Gustav Landauer, Michael Bakunin and Herbert Read with the philosophy of René Guénon, Herbert Marcuse and Jean Baudrillard; the existentialism of Karl Jaspers and Colin Wilson; the vision of Carl Jung, Oswald Spengler and Idries Shah, and the environmental insight of Derrick Jensen and Paul Shepard in a work of ideological alchemy fuelled by the ancient universal esoteric beliefs found in Sufism, Taoism and hermeticism.

"The least pessimistic book I can recall reading. It brings anarchist resistance and the spirit together in a very wide-ranging and powerful contribution". John Zerzan, author of *Future Primitive* and *Running on Emptiness*.

Also from Winter Oak

ANTIBODIES, ANARCHANGELS & OTHER ESSAYS

PAUL CUDENEC

Antibodies, Anarchangels and Other Essays brings together a selection of work by Paul Cudenec in which he calls for a new deeper level of resistance to global capitalism – one which is rooted in the collective soul. He leads us along the intertwining environmental and philosophical strands of *Antibodies*, through the passion of *Anarchangels* and *The Task* and on to an informative analysis of Gladio, a state-terrorist branch of what he terms the "plutofascist" system. Also included, alongside short pieces on Taoism and Jungian psychology, is an interview with the author, in which he explains key aspects of his approach.

"Very readable and profoundly thoughtful... Many new insights on the destructive relationship between the greater part of humanity and the planet which tries to sustain them". Peter Marshall, author of *Demanding the Impossible: A History of Anarchism*.

Also from Winter Oak

RICHARD JEFFERIES: HIS LIFE AND HIS IDEALS

HENRY S. SALT

"He was a pagan, a pantheist, a worshipper of earth and sea, and of the great sun 'burning in the heaven'; he yearned for a free, natural, fearless life of physical health and spiritual exaltation, and for a death in harmony with the life that preceded it."

So is the writer Richard Jefferies (1848-1887) described by Henry S. Salt in this study first published in 1894. The book sparked controversy at the time, as Salt – a campaigner for animal rights, vegetarianism and socialism – used it to claim Jefferies for one of his own, highlighting the social radicalism and nature-based spirituality in his subject's later writing. He demolishes the conservative presentation of Jefferies as a mere chronicler of country life and reveals him as a flawed yet inspirational figure whose best works were "unsurpassed as prose poems by anything which the English language contains". With a preface by Paul Cudenec.

Also from Winter Oak

THE STORY OF MY HEART

RICHARD JEFFERIES

"Having drunk deeply of the heaven above and felt the most glorious beauty of the day, and remembering the old, old, sea, which (as it seemed to me) was but just yonder at the edge, I now became lost, and absorbed into the being or existence of the universe. I felt down deep into the earth under, and high above into the sky, and farther still to the sun and stars. Still farther beyond the stars into the hollow of space, and losing thus my separateness of being came to seem like a part of the whole".

Richard Jefferies' masterpiece of prose-poetry expresses his sublime yearning not just for connection with nature but for spiritual transcendence. This new Winter Oak edition includes a preface by writer Paul Cudenec exploring the significance of Jefferies' work against a backdrop of disillusionment with industrial civilization and a cultural urge for the regeneration of human society.

MORE INFORMATION

To get in touch with Winter Oak please email
winteroak@greenmail.net or go to our website at
www.winteroak.org.uk.

40559262R00105

Made in the USA
Charleston, SC
10 April 2015